Mortality Rates in Middle and Low-Income Countries

Edited by Umar Bacha

Published in London, United Kingdom

IntechOpen

Supporting open minds since 2005

Mortality Rates in Middle and Low-Income Countries
http://dx.doi.org/10.5772/intechopen.95702
Edited by Umar Bacha

Contributors
Mehmet Tekin, Setegn Muche Fenta, Haile Mekonnen Fenta, Gayatri Devi Ramalingam, G. Sridevi, Jothi Priya Amirtham, Preetha Santhakumar, S. Saravanakumar, Mary Agoyi, Roland Ojo, Toyosi Afolabi, Olakunmi Ogunyemi, Sekinat Adejumobi, Adeyemi Awoniyi, Emmanuel Anongeba Anaba, Juliana Gyasi Necku, Moses Abile, Umar Bacha, Naveed Munir

First published in London, United Kingdom, 2022 by IntechOpen
IntechOpen is the global imprint of INTECHOPEN LIMITED, registered in England and Wales, registration number: 11086078, 5 Princes Gate Court, London, SW7 2QJ, United Kingdom
Printed in Croatia

British Library Cataloguing-in-Publication Data
A catalogue record for this book is available from the British Library

Additional hard and PDF copies can be obtained from orders@intechopen.com

Mortality Rates in Middle and Low-Income Countries
Edited by Umar Bacha
p. cm.
Print ISBN 978-1-83969-969-6
Online ISBN 978-1-83969-970-2
eBook (PDF) ISBN 978-1-83969-971-9

Meet the editor

Umar Bacha is an associate professor at the School of Health Sciences, University of Management and Technology, Lahore, Pakistan. He obtained a BSc (Hons) in Biochemistry and an MPhil and Ph.D. in Nutrition. He has published several research papers and authored and co-authored several books. His fields of interest are nutrient and drug interactions, nutraceuticals, and public health. Dr. Bacha has several national and international awards to his credit.

Contents

Preface

Mortality Rates in Middle and Low-Income Countries is a compilation of six chapters comprised of reviews, research works, and authors' opinions providing insight into the previous and present trends in mortality rates in different countries. The book describes causes and factors leading to high mortality and the latest developments in the field of healthcare with best practices to reduce and limit mortality in all ages. It also presents mortality and related health outcomes in economically poor countries. There are many encouraging examples where mortality rates have been reduced by some countries and thus similar approaches and interventions can be adapted by other countries to lower the mortality rate and improve the existing healthcare system.

Chapters 1 and 2 introduce determinants of mortality in various countries. Chapter 3 focuses on child mortality. Chapter 4 describes the stress and sustainable interventions such as the role of music in decreasing stress and related health outcomes. Chapter 5 describes health-seeking behaviors among cancer patients and introduces a new matrix/index of people load per hospital. Finally, Chapter 6 discusses the status of maternal and child mortality and highlights successful interventions to reduce maternal and child mortality, for example, the use of community-based birth attendants. Written by experts, this book can be adopted at various levels to bolster the quality of healthcare systems worldwide.

Umar Bacha
School of Health Sciences,
University of Management and Technology,
Lahore, Pakistan

Section 1

Determinant of Mortality

Chapter 1

Level and Determinant of Child Mortality Rate in Ethiopia

Setegn Muche Fenta and Haile Mekonnen Fenta

Abstract

Background: One of the objectives of the Sustainable Development Goals (SDG) is to diminish the under-five mortality rate and improvement in maternal health. This study aims to identify factors that affect under-five mortality based on the 2016 EDHS dataset using the multilevel count regression model. **Method:** The EDHS data have a two-level hierarchical structure, with 14,370 women nested within 11 geographical regions. Multilevel count models were employed to predict the outcomes. **Results:** The data were found to have excess zeros (53.7%); the variance (1.697) is higher than its mean (0.90). Among families of count models, the HNB model was found to be a better fit for the dataset than the others. The study revealed that a child of multiple births is 1.45 more likely to die as compared with a single birth. Babies delivered in the private sector are a 0.65 lower risk of under-five mortality compared to the babies delivered at home. **Conclusion:** Vaccination of child, family size, age of mother, antenatal visit, birth interval, birth order, contraceptive used, father education level, mother education level, father occupation, place of delivery, child twin, age first birth and religion were significantly associated with under-five mortality. The Ministry of Health should work properly to raise the awareness of parents for vaccination, family planning services and efforts should be made to improve the parental educational level.

Keywords: under five mortality, Ethiopia, hurdle negative binomial

1. Introduction

Seventeen Sustainable Development Goals (SDGs) were agreed upon by global leaders based on millennium development goals. SDG goal 3 target 3.2 is to reduce infant and under-5 mortality by 2030. The target is to drop the "neonatal mortality as low as 12 per 1000 live births and under-five Mortality to as low as 25 per thousand live births" [1]. According to UNICEF, the problem of under-five mortality requires urgent attention from the health sector. If the conditions remain as such, approximately 60 million innocent children will die until 2030 (more than half of the Ethiopian population) [2].

Every year, millions of children under 5 years of age die (WHO, 2016). In 2016, about 15,000 children still die every single day globally. The level of under-five mortality remains high in certain regions of the world. Sub-Saharan African Region continues to be the region with the highest rate of under-five mortality. In 2016, the under five-mortality rate in sub-Saharan African was 79 deaths per 1000 live births, nearly 15 times the average in developed countries [1–3].

 IntechOpen

In Ethiopia, the under-five mortality rate stands at 67 per 1000 live births, with large inequalities in her different regions. Every year, more than 257,000 children under the age of five dies [4]. If the situations continue as such, more than 3,084,000 children will die until 2030.

Most of the previous studies were done by using single-level binary logistic and survival analysis including the above studies we mentioned, but under-five mortality varies across different physical, ecological, and political structures within countries. One such contextual determinant is the regional environment [5–7]. In Ethiopia, there have been regional variations in a number of under-five mortality [8, 9]. In this study, we assume the region affects modeling the determinants of the number of under-five mortality, which may be due to the heterogeneity in regions of the study. As a result, the multilevel model approach is relatively better to determine the covariates related to under-five mortality [10, 11]. Therefore, this study was targeted to investigate the major socio-economic, demographic, health, and environmental proximate factors that might influence under-five mortality in Ethiopia with different multilevel count model approaches.

2. Methodology

The data used for this study was taken from the 2016 EDHS which is a nationally representative survey of women's age (15–49 years age) groups taken from the CSA, Ethiopia. This survey is the fourth compressive survey designed to provide estimates for the health and demographic variables of interest for the whole urban and rural areas of Ethiopia as a domain. In all of the selected households, measurements were collected from children age 0–59 months, women age 15–49 years, and men age 15–59 years old.

The main outcome variable in this study is the number of under-five death per mother. Thus, this paper attempts to include socioeconomic, demographic, health, and environmental related factors that are assumed as a potential determinant for the barriers in the number of under-five death per mother, adopted from literature reviews and their theoretical justification.

A multilevel count regression model can account for a lack of independence across levels of nested data (in this case, individual mothers nested within regions). Conventional count regression assumes that all experimental units are independent in the sense that any variable which affects the occurrence of under-five mortality has the same effect in all regions, but observations from similar environments might have shown similar behaviors as opposed to observations from a different environment. Multilevel models are used to assess whether the effects of predictors vary from region to region. The main statistical model of multilevel analysis is the HGLM, an extension of the (GLM) that includes nested random coefficients [10, 12].

The multilevel count regression model has a count outcome (number of under-five mortality). Now consider the full model equation for the two-level Poisson regression with i^{th} individual mothers is nested within the jth region. The response variable, i.e., we let Y_{ij} is the ith individual mothers in j^{th} region has under-five mortality. Using a log link function the two-level model is given by:

$$\log\left(\mu_{ij}\right) = \beta_{oj} + \sum_{l=1}^{k} \beta_{lj} x_{lij}; l = 1, 2, \ldots, k \tag{1}$$

Where $\beta_{oj} = \beta_o + U_{oj}, \beta_{lj} = \beta_1 + U_{1j}, \ldots + \beta_k + U_{kj}$.

The level-two model (1) can be rewritten as:

$$\log\left(\mu_{ij}\right) = \beta_o + \sum_{l=1}^{k} \beta_l x_{lij} + U_{oj} + \sum_{l=1}^{k} U_{lj} x_{lij} \tag{2}$$

Where $x_{ij} = \left(x_{1ij}, x_{2ij}, \ldots x_{kij}\right)$ represent the first and the second level covariates, $\beta = (\beta_0, \beta_1, \ldots \beta_k)$ are regression coefficients, $U_{oj}, U_{1j}, \ldots\ldots U_{kj}$ are the random effect of the model parameter at level two (region level). It assumed that the $U_{oj}, U_{1j}, \ldots\ldots U_{kj}$ follow a normal distribution with mean zero and variance ${\sigma_u}^2$ [13]. Without $U_{oj}, U_{1j}, \ldots\ldots U_{kj}$, Eq. (2) can be considered as a single-level Poisson regression model.

2.1 Empty model

The empty two-level model for a count outcome variable refers to a population of groups (level-two units) and specifies the probability distribution for group-dependent μ_{ij} in $Y_{ij} = \mu_{ij} + \varepsilon_{ij}$ without taking further explanatory variables into account. We focused on the model that specifies the transformed $\log\left(\mu_{ij}\right)$ to have a normal distribution. This is expressed, for a general link function $\log(\mu)$, by the formula.

$$\log\left(\mu_{ij}\right) = \beta_0 + U_{oj} \tag{3}$$

Where β_o is a fixed coefficient and U_{oj} is a random term that is independently and normally distributed with mean 0 and variance ${\sigma_u}^2$ (random intercept variance) [14]. This model is also named as empty Poisson regression model (null model). A null model contains only a response variable, and no explanatory variables other than an intercept. Thus, ${\sigma_u}^2$ measures regional variations of under-five mortality.

2.2 The random intercept model

A random intercepts model is a model in which intercepts are allowed to vary. The scores on the dependent variable for each individual observation are predicted by the intercept that varies across regions, but the relationship between explanatory and response variables cannot differ between groups. The random intercept model expresses the natural log of μ_{ij}, as a sum of a linear function of the explanatory variables. That is,

$$\begin{aligned}\log\left(\mu_{ij}\right) &= \beta_{0j} + \beta_1 x_{1ij} + \beta_2 x_{2ij} + \ldots. + \beta_k x_{kij} \\ &= \beta_{oj} + \sum_{l=1}^{k} \beta_l x_{lij}\end{aligned} \tag{4}$$

Where the intercept term β_{oj} is allowed to vary across the regions and is given by the sum of an average intercept β_0 and regions-dependent deviations U_{oj}, that is.

$$\beta_{oj} = \beta_o + U_{oj}$$

As a result, we have:

$$\log\left(\mu_{ij}\right) = \beta_o + \sum_{l=1}^{k} \beta_l x_{lij} + U_{oj} \tag{5}$$

Note that the above equation $\beta_o + \sum_{l=1}^{k} \beta_l x_{lij}$ is the fixed part of the model. The remaining U_{oj} is called the random part of the model. It is assumed that the random part of U_{oj} are mutually independent and normally distributed with mean zero and variance σ_{uo}^2.

2.3 The random coefficients model

A random slopes model is the slopes are different across regions. In other words, the relationship between an explanatory variable and the response is different across all regions. If we fit a model based on the same predictors on the response variable for all regions separately, we may obtain different intercepts and slopes for each region. Now consider a model with group-specific regressions, on a single level one explanatory variable X,

$$\log\left(\mu_{ij}\right) = \beta_{0j} + \beta_{1j} x_{1ij} \tag{6}$$

The intercepts β_{oj} as well as the regression coefficients or slopes, β_{1j} are group dependent. These group dependent coefficients can be split into an average coefficient and the group dependent deviation:

$$\beta_{oj} = \beta_o + U_{oj}$$

$$\beta_{1j} = \beta_1 + U_{1j}$$

Substitution into (6) leads to the model

$$\log\left(\mu_{ij}\right) = \left(\beta_o + U_{oj}\right) + \left(\beta_1 + U_{1j}\right) x_{1ij} = \beta_o + \beta_1 x_{1ij} + U_{oj} + U_{1j} x_{1ij} \tag{7}$$

There are two random group effects, the random intercept U_{oj} and the random slope U_{1j}. It is assumed that the level two residuals U_{oj} and U_{1j} have both zero mean given the value of the explanatory variable X. Thus, β_1 is the average regression coefficient like β_0 is the average intercept. The first part of Eq. (7) $\beta_o + \beta_1 x_{1ij}$ is called the fixed part of the model whereas the second part $U_{oj} + U_{1j} x_{1ij}$ is called the random part of the model.

The term $U_{oj} + U_{1j} x_{1ij}$ can be regarded as a random interaction between group and predictors (X). This model implies that the groups are characterized by two random effects: their intercept and their slope. These two groups' effects U_{oj} and U_{1j} will not be independent. Further, it is assumed that, for different groups, the pairs of random effects $\left(U_{oj}, U_{1j}\right)$ are independent and identically distributed. Thus, the variances and covariance of the level-two random effects $\left(U_{oj}, U_{1j}\right)$ are denoted by:

$$Var\left(U_{oj}\right) = \sigma_{00} = \sigma_0^2$$

$$Var\left(U_{1j}\right) = \sigma_{11} = \sigma_1^2$$

$$Cov\left(U_{oj}, U_{1j}\right) = \sigma_{01}$$

The model for a single explanatory variable discussed above can be extended by including more variables that have random effects.

2.4 Multilevel negative binomial regression model

The hierarchical study design or the data collection procedure, over-desperation, and lack of independence may occur simultaneously, which render the standard NB model inadequate. To account for the over-desperation and the inherent correlation of observations, a class of multilevel NB regression models with random effects is presented. The multilevel NB model is then generalized to cope with a more complex correlation structure. The multilevel NB model derives by allowing for between regional random variation of the expected number of under-five mortality μ_{ij}.

$$\ln \mu_{ij} = \eta_{ij} + e_{ij} \tag{8}$$

Where $\text{cov}\left(e_{ij}, \eta_{ij}\right) = 0$ and $\exp\left(e_{ij}\right)$ follows a gamma probability distribution, $\Gamma(v)$, with mean 1 and variance $\alpha = v_{-1}$. Integrating concerning e_{ij} [15] the resulting probability distribution

$$p\left(Y_{ij} = y_{ij}\right) = \frac{\exp\left(-\exp\left(\eta_{ij} + e_{ij}\right)\exp\left(\eta_{ij} + e_{ij}\right)^{y_{ij}}\right.}{y_{ij}!} \tag{9}$$

One version of the multilevel negative binomial regression model is obtained;

$$p\left(Y_{ij} = y_{ij}\right) = \frac{\Gamma\left(y_{ij} + v\right) v^{v} \mu_{ij}{}^{* y_{ij}}}{y_{ij}!\Gamma(v)\left(v + \mu_{ij}{}^{*}\right)^{v + y_{ij}}} y_{ij} = 0, 1, 2.. ... \tag{10}$$

With mean and variance given, respectively, as follows:

The multilevel negative binomial regression model gives the expected mean of a number of under-five mortality. $E\left(Y_{ij}\right) = \mu_{ij}{}^{*} = \log\left(\eta_{ij}\right)$. Its variance is given by $\text{var}\left(y_{ij}\right) = \mu_{ij} + \alpha\mu_{ij}^{2}$. Where $\eta_{ij} = \beta_{0j} + \beta_{1j}x_{1ij} + \beta_{2j}x_{2ij} + \ldots. + \beta_{kj}x_{kij}$

2.5 Multilevel ZIP regression model

ZIP regression is useful for modeling count data with excess zeros, but because of hierarchical study design or the data collection procedure, zero-inflation and correlation may occur simultaneously [16]. Multilevel ZIP regression is used to overcome these problems. Let Y_{ij} be a count say, the number of under-five mortalities the ith mother in the jth region follows a multilevel ZIP distribution:

$$p\left(Y_{ij} = y_{j}\right) = \begin{cases} \pi_{ij} + \left(1 - \pi_{ij}\right)\exp\left(-\mu_{ij}\right), & if\, y_{ij} = 0 \\ \left(1 - \pi_{ij}\right)\dfrac{\exp\left(-\mu_{ij}\right)\mu_{ij}{}^{y_{ij}}}{y_{ij}!}, & if\, y_{ij} = 1, 2, \ldots \ldots \end{cases} \quad 0 \le \pi_{ij} \le 1 \tag{11}$$

Recently, the ZIP regression model has been extended to the random effects setting, where by random components w_j and u_j are incorporated within the logistic and Poisson linear predictors to account for the dependence of observations within j^{th} region [16]. These random effects ZIP models are region-specific in the sense that the random effects w_j and u_j so introduced are specific to the jth region. In the following, a multi-level ZIP regression model is developed to handle correlated count data with extra zeros.

Without loss of generality, consider the two-level hierarchical situation where Y_{ij} represents the ith observation of under-five mortality the jth individual region $(i = 1, 2, \ldots\ldots, n)$ and $(j = 1, 2, \ldots\ldots, m)$. Let m be the total number of individuals in each region and $\sum_{j=1}^{m}\sum_{i=1}^{ni} ni$ gives the total number of observations. The observations may be taken to be independent between regions, but certain within-household and within-individual correlations are anticipated, which can be modeled explicitly through random effects attached to the linear predictors:

$$\log\left(\mu_{ij}\right) = \beta_o + \sum_{l=1}^{k} \beta_l x_{lij} + U_{oj} + \sum_{l=1}^{k} U_{lj} x_{lij} \tag{12}$$

$$\log it\left(\pi_{ij}\right) = \log\left(\frac{\pi_{ij}}{1-\pi_{ij}}\right) = \gamma_o + \sum_{l=1}^{k} \gamma_l z_{lij} + W_{oj} + \sum_{l=1}^{k} W_{lj} z_{lij} \tag{13}$$

Here, the covariates X_{ij} and Z_{ij} appearing in the respective Poisson and logistic components are not necessarily the same, β and γ are the corresponding vectors of regression coefficients [17, 18]. For simplicity of presentation, the random effect u and w assumed to be independent and normally distributed with mean zero and variance ${\sigma_u}^2$ and ${\sigma_w}^2$ respectively.

2.6 Multilevel ZINB regression model

Multilevel ZINB regression model is proposed for over-dispersed count data with extra zeros. A multilevel ZINB regression incorporating random effects to account for data dependency and over-dispersion is used [17]. Let $Y_{ij}(i = 1, 2, \ldots\ldots, n; j = 1, 2, \ldots\ldots, m)$ be a count say, the under-five mortality of the ith mother in j^{th} region follows a ZINB distribution:

$$p\left(Y_{ij} = y_{ij}\right) = \begin{cases} \pi_{ij} + \dfrac{\left(1-\pi_{ij}\right)}{\left(1+\alpha\mu_{ij}\right)^{-\frac{1}{\alpha}}}, & if\ y_{ij} = 0 \\ 1 - \pi_{ij}\dfrac{\Gamma\left(y_{ij} + 1/\alpha\right)}{y_{ij}!\Gamma(1/\alpha)}\left(1+\alpha\mu_{ij}\right)^{-\frac{1}{\alpha}}\left(1+\dfrac{1}{\alpha\mu_{ij}}\right)^{-y_{ij}}, & if\ y_{ij} > 0 \end{cases} \quad 0 \le \pi_{ij} \le 1$$

In my study, mothers are nested in regions and the number of under-five mortality is taken to be the response variable. Let n be the total number of individuals in each region and $\sum_{j=1}^{m}\sum_{i=1}^{ni} ni$ gives the total number of observations. Hence the responses of under-five mortality which belong to the different regions are independent, while they are correlated for those who live in the same region. This dependence can be modeled explicitly by considering suitable random effects in the linear predictor.

Negative binomial models for counts permit μ to depend on explanatory variables. Then the two-level ZINB regression model can be expressed in vector form as:

$$\log\left(\mu_{ij}\right) = \beta_o + \sum_{l=1}^{k} \beta_l x_{lij} + U_{oj} + \sum_{l=1}^{k} U_{lj} x_{lij} \tag{14}$$

$$\log it(\pi_{ij}) = \log\left(\frac{\pi_{ij}}{1-\pi_{ij}}\right) = \gamma_o + \sum_{l=1}^{k} \gamma_l z_{lij} + W_{oj} + \sum_{l=1}^{k} W_{lj} z_{lij} \tag{15}$$

Here, the covariates X_{ij} and Z_{ij} appearing in the respective negative binomial and logistic components are not necessarily the same, β and γ are the corresponding vectors of regression coefficients [17, 18]. The vectors w_j and u_j denote the region-specific random effects for simplicity of presentation. The random effect u and w assumed to be independent and normally distributed with mean zero and variance ${\sigma_u}^2$ and ${\sigma_w}^2$ respectively.

2.7 Multilevel hurdle regression model

The hurdle model [19] has mostly been adopted to conduct an economic analysis of healthcare utilization. The hierarchical study design or the data collection procedure, zero-inflation, and lack of independence may occur simultaneously, which the standard Hurdle Poisson regression model is inadequate. To account for the preponderance of zero counts and the inherent correlation of observations, a class of multilevel Hurdle Poisson regression models with random effects is presented. In this study, suppose that Y_{ij} is the number of under-five mortality in i^{th} mother in the jth region. Then multilevel Poisson Hurdle model can be written as follows

$$p\left(Y_{ij} = y_{ij}\right) = \begin{cases} \pi_{ij} & if\, y_{ij} = 0 \\ (1-\pi_{ij}) \dfrac{\exp\left(-\mu_{ij}\right) {\mu_{ij}}^{y_{ij}}}{\left(1-\exp\left(-\mu_{ij}\right)\right) y_{ij}!} & if\, y_{ij} = 1, 2, \ldots\ldots \quad 0 \le \pi_{ij} \le 1 \end{cases} \tag{16}$$

In the regression setting, both the mean μ_{ij} and zero proportion π_{ij} parameters are related to the covariate vectors x_{ij} and z_{ij} respectively. Moreover, responses within the same region are likely to be correlated. To accommodate the inherent correlation, random effects u_j and w_j are incorporated in the linear predictors η_{ij} for the Poisson part and ξ_{ij} for the zero part. The

Hurdle Poisson mixed regression model is

$$\eta_{ij} = \log\left(\mu_{ij}\right) = {x_{ij}}^T \beta + u_j \tag{17}$$

$$\xi_{ij} = \log\left(\frac{\pi_{ij}}{1-\pi_{ij}}\right) = {z_{ij}}^T \gamma + w_j \tag{18}$$

Where β and γ are the corresponding $(p+1) \times 1$ and $(q+1) \times 1$ vector of regression coefficients. The random effects u_j and w_j are assumed to be independent and normally distributed with mean 0 and variance ${\sigma_u}^2$ and ${\sigma_w}^2$, respectively [12].

3. Result and discussion

3.1 Result

A total of 14,370 women from all the 11 regions of the country were included and 7720 (53.3%) of the mothers have not faced any under-five death and only 78

(0.5%) of them lost 7 of their under-five children. Since there is a large number of zero outcomes. Additional screening of the number of under-five death calculated showed that the variance (1.697) is greater than the mean (0.9) indicating over-dispersion. This is an indication that the data could be fitted better by count data models which takes into account excess zeroes (**Table 1**).

The mean numbers under-five death for uneducated fathers (1.1063) are higher than fathers with secondary and above education (0.353) and the mean number of under-five death that children who are delivered at home (1.0995) have highest than those delivered in health institutions (0.2507). Moreover, the highest and lowest mean number of child death are observed for a child of birth order of four and above and first birth order (1.1189 and 0.6167) respectively.

The result also showed that the breastfeeding mothers have a lower mean number of under-five deaths (0.6254) and the highest mean number of under-five death is occurred children born less than or equal to 24 months (1.0568) (**Table 2**)

3.2 Multilevel count analysis of the data

3.2.1 Test of heterogeneity

Comparisons of multilevel models with their single-level count model, with LRT statistic given in **Table 3**. The values of LRT's for each model are larger than the critical value $X^2_\alpha(2) = 5.99$ with p-value <0.05. Thus, there is evidence of heterogeneity of under-five death across regions. It also observed that multilevel count regression model is best fit over the single level count regression models (**Table 3**).

3.2.2 The goodness of fit and model selection criteria

The multilevel HNB regression model has a smaller value in deviance, AIC, and BIC than the other model. Consequently, we conclude that in this study multilevel HNB regression model is better than the other model (**Table 4**).

Number of death	Frequency	Percent
0	7720	53.7
1	3314	23.1
2	1773	12.3
3	798	5.6
4	413	2.9
5	198	1.4
6	76	0.5
7	78	0.5
Total	14,370	100
Mean	0.90	
Variance	1.67	

Table 1.
Frequency distribution of the number of under-5 deaths per mother.

Variables	Categories	Mean	Std. D	Women
Region	Tigray	0.7333	1.1375	1376
	Afar	1.1227	1.4106	1475
	Amhara	1.0535	1.3547	1478
	Oromia	0.8052	1.2342	2059
	Somali	0.9174	1.3566	1937
	Benishan	1.2054	1.5991	1251
	SNNPR	0.9580	1.2749	1809
	Gambela	0.6487	0.8761	928
	Harari	0.6169	0.9381	744
	Addis Abeba	0.2424	0.5738	524
	Dire Dawa	1.0292	1.4637	789
Residence	Urban	0.5816	1.0940	2512
	Rural	0.9645	1.3251	11,858
Education level of father	No education	1.1063	1.4265	8250
	Primary	0.7457	1.1365	4101
	Sec. and above	0.3531	0.7016	2019
Education level of mother	No education	1.1093	1.4111	9932
	Primary	0.4861	0.8710	3197
	Sec. and above	0.2627	0.5973	1241
Father's occupation	Not working	1.0675	1.4414	2579
	Had working	0.8604	1.2587	11,791
Marital status	Married	0.8745	1.2812	13,086
	Others	1.1324	1.4152	1284
Age of first birth	<=16	1.1596	1.4613	6065
	>16	0.7062	1.1222	8305
Type of birth	Single	0.8556	1.2596	13,813
	Multiple	1.9390	1.6889	557
Place of delivery	Home	1.0995	1.3804	10,884
	Public sector	0.2691	0.6788	3107
	Private sector	0.2507	0.5846	379
Breastfeeding	No	1.2331	1.4524	6436
	Yes	0.6254	1.0793	7934
Birth order	first birth	0.6167	1.0082	3206
	2–3	0.7851	1.2032	4705
	4 and above	1.1189	1.4421	6459
Contraceptive used	No	0.9965	1.3607	10,976
	Yes	0.5775	0.9940	3394
Vaccination of child	No	1.0140	1.3573	11,881
	Yes	0.3419	0.7256	2489

Variables	Categories	Mean	Std. D	Women
Antenatal visit	No visit	1.1856	1.4147	9658
	1–3	0.3599	0.7550	2092
	4 and above	0.2649	0.6638	2620
Previous birth interval	0–24 months	1.0568	1.4120	7129
	25–36 months	0.9061	1.2517	3407
	>36 months	0.5939	1.0272	3834

Table 2.
Summary statistics of predictor variables related to under-five death in Ethiopia.

Test	Multilevel Models					
	Poisson	NB	ZIP	ZINB	HP	HNB
LRT	111.34	107.8	111.2	105.2	133.86	130.48

Table 3.
Likelihood ratio test value for multilevel and ordinary count model.

Criteria	Multilevel Models					
	Poisson	NB	ZIP	ZINB	HP	HNB
Deviance	30200.4	30177.7	29661.7	29659.8	29331.1	**29312.3**
AIC	30246.4	30225.7	29745.7	29741.8	29415.1	**29398.3**
BIC	30420.6	30407.4	30063.8	30052.2	29733.2	**29723.9**

Table 4.
Model selection criteria for the multilevel count regression models.

Model selection	Intercept-only	Random intercept	Random coefficient
Deviance	37,263	29,312	**29042.9**
AIC	37,273	29,398	**29186.9**
BIC	37,311	29,724	**29,705**

Table 5.
Summary results of multilevel HNB model selection criteria.

3.2.3 Model comparisons in multilevel HNB model

The smallest deviance, AIC, and BIC is the better to fit. The result indicated that the random coefficient model is a better fit as compared to the empty model with random intercept and the random intercept and fixed-effect model (**Table 5**).

3.2.4 Results of random coefficient HNB model

From **Table 6** in the random effect for truncated count part, estimates for intercepts and the slopes vary significantly at 5% significance level, which implies that there is a considerable variation in the effects of family size, age of mother and

Estimation of Fixed effect count part							
	Estimate	S.E	Z value	P-value	IRR	95% CI for RR	
						Lower	Upper
Intercept	−1.5889	0.2300	−6.908	0.0001	0.204	0.130	0.320
Vaccination child (No) (Ref)							
Yes	−0.3219	0.0635	−5.071	0.0001	0.725	0.640	0.821
Family size	−0.0384	0.0184	−2.088	0.03681	0.962	0.928	0.998
Age of mother	0.0535	0.0044	12.229	0.0001	1.055	1.046	1.064
Antenatal visit (No)							
1–3	−0.2352	0.0662	−3.552	0.0003	0.790	0.694	0.900
4 and above	−0.2406	0.0740	−3.249	0.0011	0.786	0.680	0.909
PB interval (≤24 months)							
25–36 months	−0.2429	0.0298	−8.165	0.0001	0.784	0.740	0.831
37 and above	−0.3700	0.0361	−10.245	0.0001	0.691	0.643	0.741
Birth order (First)							
2–3	0.3828	0.0419	9.141	0.0001	1.466	1.351	1.592
4 and above	0.4611	0.0398	11.575	0.0001	1.586	1.467	1.715
Religion (Orthodox)							
Muslim	0.1909	0.0429	4.452	0.0001	1.210	1.113	1.316
Others	0.1535	0.0526	2.916	0.00354	1.166	1.052	1.293
Contraceptive use (No)							
Yes	−0.1742	0.0382	−4.558	0.0001	0.840	0.779	0.905
Father's education (No education)							
Primary	−0.0393	0.0318	−1.235	0.21688	0.962	0.903	1.023
Secondary or above	−0.3331	0.0749	−4.449	0.0001	0.716	0.619	0.830
Mother's education (No education)							
Primary	−0.3224	0.1085	−2.973	0.0001	0.724	0.586	0.896
Secondary or above	−0.2525	0.2301	−1.098	0.27240	0.777	0.495	1.220
Father occupation (No)							
Had working	0.0920	0.0304	3.023	0.00250	1.096	1.033	1.164
P delivery (home)							
Public sector	−0.0451	0.0676	−0.667	0.50487	0.956	0.837	1.091
private sector	−0.4296	0.2063	−2.083	0.03724	0.651	0.434	0.975
Child Twin (single)							
Multiple	0.3746	0.0390	9.607	0.0001	1.454	1.347	1.570
AMF birth (≤16)							
17 and above	−0.3486	0.0244	−14.270	0.0001	0.706	0.673	0.740
Log(theta)	6.69	0.8435	7.93	0.0001			
Estimation of Random effect truncated count part							
Intercept ($\hat{\sigma}^2_{u0}$)	0.450	0.201	2.24	0.0250	0.1347	1.4527	
Family size ($\hat{\sigma}^2_{u2}$)	0.175	0.086	2.035	0.0418	0.0736	0.4130	

Estimation of Fixed effect count part							
	Estimate	**S.E**	**Z value**	**P-value**	**IRR**	**95% CI for RR**	
						Lower	**Upper**
Age of mother ($\hat{\sigma}^2_{u3}$)	0.100	0.042	2.38	0.0173	0.0365	0.2354	
Mother's education ($\hat{\sigma}^2_{u8}$)	0.102	0.037	2.76	0.0052	0.0382	0.2701	
Estimation of Fixed effect for zero-inflated part							
	Estimate	**S.E**	**z value**	**P-value**	**OR**	**95% CI for RR**	
						Lower	**Upper**
Intercept	3.1270	0.2914	10.730	0.0001	22.81	12.882	40.373
Vaccination child (No)							
Yes	0.5298	0.1276	4.153	0.0001	1.699	1.323	2.181
Family size	0.2215	0.0246	9.018	0.0001	1.248	1.189	1.309
Age of mother	−0.1836	0.0072	−25.503	0.0001	0.832	0.821	0.844
Antenatal visit (No)							
1–3	0.6961	0.0660	10.539	0.0001	2.006	1.762	2.283
4 and above	0.8253	0.0714	11.560	0.0001	2.283	1.985	2.626
PB interval (≤24 months)							
25–36 months	0.5637	0.0544	10.361	0.0001	1.757	1.579	1.955
37 and above	1.2763	0.0575	22.211	0.0001	3.583	3.202	4.011
Contraceptive use (No)							
Yes	0.2636	0.0571	4.616	0.0001	1.302	1.164	1.456
Father's education (No education)							
Primary	−0.0760	0.0533	−1.425	0.154	0.927	0.835	1.029
Secondary or above	0.1388	0.0845	1.644	0.100	1.149	0.974	1.356
Mother's education (No education)							
Primary	0.1262	0.0595	2.121	0.033	1.135	1.010	1.275
Secondary or above	0.2165	0.1131	1.915	0.055	1.242	0.995	1.550
Father occupation (No)							
Had working	−0.3287	0.0620	−5.302	0.0001	0.720	0.638	0.813
P delivery (home) (ref.)							
Public sector	0.7722	0.1884	4.099	0.0001	2.164	1.496	3.131
Private sector	0.4454	0.3847	1.158	0.0001	1.561	0.735	3.318
Child Twin (single)							
Multiple	−1.4608	0.2398	−6.093	0.0001	0.232	0.145	0.371
AMF birth (≤16)							
17 and above	1.0501	0.0469	22.404	0.0001	2.858	2.607	3.133
Estimation of random effect for zero-inflated part							
Intercept ($\hat{\sigma}^2_{w0}$)	0.668	0.234	2.855	0.0043		0.1681	2.6562
Vaccination child ($\hat{\sigma}^2_{w1}$)	0.161	0.058	2.776	0.0055		0.0185	0.5704
Family size ($\hat{\sigma}^2_{w2}$)	0.146	0.070	2.086	0.0369		0.0566	0.3733

Estimation of Fixed effect for zero-inflated part							
	Estimate	S.E	z value	P-value	OR	95% CI for RR	
						Lower	Upper
Age of mother ($\hat{\sigma}^2_{w3}$)	0.042	0.015	2.8	0.0051		0.0083	0.2096
Place of delivery ($\hat{\sigma}^2_{w8}$)	0.333	0.161	2.068	0.0385		0.1234	0.8987
Child Twin ($\hat{\sigma}^2_{w9}$)	0.463	0.212	2.184	0.0284		0.0707	1.8771

Table 6.
The results of random coefficients HNB model.

mother's education these variables differ significantly across the regions. The value of 0.45, 0.175, 0.100, and 0.102 are the estimated variance of intercept (region), family size, age of mother, and mother's education respectively.

The fixed part of **Table 6** shows vaccination of children has a significant impact on the number of non-zero under-five death per mother. The expected number of non-zero under-five death for vaccinated children are decreased by a factor of 0.73 as compared with non-vaccinated children.

Unexpectedly, the findings of this study also showed that family size is a significant determinant of under-death. The risk of under-five death increases as family size decreases. For a unit increased family size, then the expected number of non-zero under-five death per mother is decreased by 0.04%. And also, mother's current age is a significant positive association with under-five mortality. Particularly, with each yearly increase in the age of mother, the expected number of non-zero under-five death is increased by 0.06%.

The result also revealed that the expected number of non-zero under-five death whose mothers visited at least 4 times during pregnancy is 0.79 times lower compared to child whose mothers who have not received any antenatal check during pregnancy.

This study found that preceding birth interval has a significant negative association with under-five mortality. The expected number of non-zero under-five death with children born more than 36 months after the previous birth decreased by 31 percent relative to children born less than 2 years after the previous birth. In addition to this as birth order increases the under-five mortality shown an increase. The expected number of non-zero under-five deaths with children's birth order 4 and above is increased by 59% as compared to the first order.

The finding of this study also revealed that mother's and father's levels of education have a significant factor in the number of under-five death. The expected number of non-zero under-five death for mothers with primary education is 0.724 times lower as compared to those with non-educated. Likewise, the expected number of non-zero under-five death for fathers with secondary and above education is 0.716 times lower as compared to those with non-educated (**Table 6**).

The random effect for the logit part also shows that estimates for intercepts and slopes vary significantly, which suggests that there is considerable variation in the effects of vaccination of child, family size, age of mother, place of delivery, and child twins, these variables differ significantly across the regions. The value of 0.688, 0.161, 0.146, 0.042, 0.333, and 0.463 are the estimated variance of intercept (region), vaccination of child, family size, age of mother, place of delivery, and child twins respectively (**Table 6**).

The fixed part of zero-inflated HNB model indicted that the estimated odds that the number of under-five death becomes zero with vaccinated children is 1.70 times as compared to non-vaccinated children. An increase in family size by 1 result, the estimated odds that the number of under-five death becomes zero is increased by 1.25. Similarly, the age of mother increase in by a year, the estimated odds that the number of under-five death becomes zero is decreased by 17%.

The result also revealed that the estimated odds that the number of under-five death becomes zero with mothers visit 4 and above is 2.28 times higher as compared to mothers who have not received any antenatal visit during pregnancy. In addition to, the estimated odds that the number of under-five death becomes zero for those children born with preceding birth intervals of more than 36 months is 3.58 times children born with preceding birth intervals of fewer than 24 months. The study also found that the employment status of a father is found to have an association with under-five mortality. The odds of the number of under-five death becomes zero with children born from fathers who have to work is 0.72 times fathers without work. Moreover, estimated odds that the number of under-five death among mothers who are used contraceptives is 1.30 times more than as compared to mothers who were not used contraceptive (**Table 6**).

3.3 Discussion of the results

In this study, we have examined the influence of particular social, economic, and demographic characteristics of mothers on under-five mortality in Ethiopia. Results showed that several factors are implicated in under-five mortality.

The level of parental education emerged as a strong predictor of under-five mortality, that is, the mortality rate decreases with an increase in parental education level. This result is in line with the previous study that, the higher the level of maternal and father education, the lower child mortality [20–23]. The risk of under-five death associated with multiple births is very high relative to single births and this study is similar to the previous studies that birth type to be linked with under-five child death as multiple births are associated with a higher risk of child mortality [9, 21, 23, 24]. The result also showed that under-five mortality is decreased as the length of preceding birth interval increased. This finding is similar to Gebretsadik and Gabreyohannes [21], Bereka and Habtewold [24], and Getachew and Bekele [25].

The finding of the study revealed that the death of under-five children from mothers using contraceptive is significantly less than children from non-contraceptive methods using mothers. The result is in accordance with Getachew and Bekele [25] and Bedada [26]. Those vaccinated children are lower risk of mortality than that of non-vaccinated children. Similar result was observed in another study done by Berhie and Yirtaw [9].

Mother's age at first birth is negatively correlated with under-five mortality that decreased the risk of under-five mortality as increase mother's age at first birth. The estimated result also shows that mothers age at first birth increases reduced the risk of under-five mortality and mothers born their first child at a younger age face high under-five mortality risk which is similar to the previous studies conducted by different scholars [22–26]. In addition to this, the study reported that for every unit increase in the ages of mother, the risk of under-five mortality increases, and this is similar to the findings of Yaya et al. [22] and Alam et al. [23]. Further, the result of this study indicated that the religion of respondents has significantly associated with under-five death with those who practice Islamic and those who practice other religions having higher chances of experiencing under-five death compared to those who practice Orthodox Christianity religions. This is consistent with the study of Yaya et al. [22].

The study showed that children born from working fathers have a higher risk of mortality than non-working fathers. This finding is consistent with Getachew and Bekele [25] additionally, increase the number of antenatal visits during pregnancy is reduce the risk of under-five mortality and this finding is confirmed by the previous researches [25]. Children born in the public and private sectors are at lower risk than those born at home. This might be due to the proper health care and attention they received during and after delivery. This has been confirmed by different studies [24, 25, 27].

The study also revealed that household size is an important variable that affects the number of under-five mortality. Amazingly, as household size increases the risk of under-five mortality significantly decreased. This result is consistent with Berhie and Yirtaw [9], Alam et al. [23], Bedada [26], and Ahmed et al. [28]. Birth order increases the under-five mortality also increases and this result is consistent with the literature reviewed and contribution from different studies on birth order [9, 24, 28].

4. Conclusions and recommendations

The purpose of this study was to identify, socioeconomic demographic, health, and environmental related determinants and to assess regional variation of a number of under-five mortality per mother in Ethiopia. The descriptive results showed that 53.7% of mothers have not experienced under-five death and only 0.5% of them lost 7 of their under-five children.

In multilevel count regression analysis, individual mothers are considered as nested within the various regions in Ethiopia. As a first step in the multilevel approach, the likelihood ratio test is applied to see if there are differences in the number of under-five death among the regions. The test suggested that, the number of under-five death varies among regions and multilevel count model fit better than the single level count model. Among the six multilevel count regression model, multilevel HNB model is the best to account for the heterogeneity of the number of under-five mortalities per mother among regions of Ethiopia.

From the three multilevel HNB regressions models, the random coefficients model provided the best fit for a number of under-five death per mother. In fixed part of random coefficients HNB model the variables like mother's age, education level of father, father's occupation, family size, age of mother at first birth, religion, vaccination of child, contraceptive use, birth order, preceding birth interval, child twin, place of delivery and antenatal visit have statistically significant effect on under-five mortality. The random part of multilevel HNB model also revealed that under-five deaths per mother differ among regions of the country in terms of mother's education, family size, ages of mother, place of delivery, vaccination of child, and type of birth. As a result, this study proposes that all regions need to have separate estimates of HNB regressions for all 11 geographical regions.

Based on the findings of the study, we forward the following possible recommendations:

1. Policies and programs aimed at addressing regional variations in under-five mortality must be formulated and their implementation must be vigorously pursued. To achieve this, while under-five mortality reduction measures which have worked to some extent in the Affar, Amhara, Benshangul-Gumuz, SNNP and DireDawa must be strengthened to achieve more results in the region, these measures could be extrapolated and applied in the remaining regions of the country. Such measures include having hospital delivery, attending prenatal care, vaccination of child, etc.

2. Efforts are needed to extend educational programmers aimed at educating mothers on the benefits of the antenatal check, age of first birth, spacing birth

interval, vaccination of child, and place of delivery to reduce under-five mortality.

3. The concerned body should work closely with both the private sector and civil society to teach households to have sufficient knowledge and awareness on under-five mortality and mechanisms of reduction and to make children very well.

4. Further studies should be conducted by taking three or four-level count regression into account to assess the variation of under-five mortality across enumeration areas and regional levels.

Author details

Setegn Muche Fenta[1,2*] and Haile Mekonnen Fenta[1,2]

1 Department of Statistics, College of Science, Debre Tabor University, Ethiopia

2 Department of Statistics, College of Science, Bahir Dar University, Ethiopia

*Address all correspondence to: setegn14@gmail.com

References

[1] You D et al. Global, regional, and national levels and trends in under-5 mortality between 1990 and 2015, with scenario-based projections to 2030: A systematic analysis by the UN Inter-agency Group for Child Mortality Estimation. The Lancet. 2015;**386** (10010):2275-2286

[2] Hug L, Sharrow D, You D. Levels & trends in child mortality: Report 2017. In: Estimates Developed by the UN Inter-agency Group for Child Mortality Estimation. 2017

[3] WHO. Children: Reducing Mortality. 2017

[4] USAID. Maternal, Neonatal and Child Health in Ethiopia. 2018

[5] Antai D. Regional inequalities in under-5 mortality in Nigeria: A population-based analysis of individual- and community-level determinants. Population Health Metrics. 2011;**9**(1):6

[6] Montgomery MR, Hewett PC. Urban poverty and health in developing countries: Household and neighborhood effects. Demography. 2005;**42**(3):397-425

[7] Wang L. Health Outcomes in Low-income Countries and Policy Implications: Empirical Findings from Demographic and Health Surveys. Vol. 2831. World Bank, Environment Department; 2002

[8] EDHS. Ethiopian Demographic and Health Survey. 2016

[9] Berhie KA, Yirtaw TG. Statistical analysis on the determinants of under five mortality in Ethiopia. American Journal of Theoretical and Applied Statistics. 2017;**6**(1):10-21

[10] Goldstein H. Multilevel Statistical Models. Vol. 922. John Wiley & Sons; 2011

[11] Hox JJ, Moerbeek M, van de Schoot R. Multilevel Analysis: Techniques and Applications. Routledge; 2010

[12] Harvey G. Multilevel Statistical Models. 2003

[13] Snijders T, Bosker R. Multilevel Modeling: An Introduction to Basic and Advanced Multilevel Modeling. 1999

[14] Sturman MC. Multiple approaches to analyzing count data in studies of individual differences: The propensity for type I errors, illustrated with the case of absenteeism prediction. Educational and Psychological Measurement. 1999;**59**(3):414-430

[15] Cameron AC, Trivedi PK. Econometric models based on count data. Comparisons and applications of some estimators and tests. Journal of Applied Econometrics. 1986;**1**(1):29-53

[16] Lee AH et al. Multi-level zero-inflated Poisson regression modelling of correlated count data with excess zeros. Statistical Methods in Medical Research. 2006;**15**(1):47-61

[17] Moghimbeigi A et al. Multilevel zero-inflated negative binomial regression modeling for over-dispersed count data with extra zeros. Journal of Applied Statistics. 2008;**35**(10):1193-1202

[18] Meng XL, Van Dyk D. The EM algorithm—An old folk-song sung to a fast new tune. Journal of the Royal Statistical Society, Series B: Statistical Methodology. 1997;**59**(3):511-567

[19] Mullahy J. Specification and testing of some modified count data models. Journal of Econometrics. 1986;**33**(3): 341-365

[20] Khan JR, Awan N. A comprehensive analysis on child mortality and its

determinants in Bangladesh using frailty models. Archives of Public Health. 2017; **75**(1):58

[21] Gebretsadik S, Gabreyohannes E. Determinants of under-five mortality in high mortality regions of Ethiopia: An analysis of the 2011 Ethiopia Demographic and Health Survey Data. International Journal of Population Research. 2016;**2016**

[22] Yaya S et al. Prevalence and determinants of childhood mortality in Nigeria. BMC Public Health. 2017;**17**(1): 485

[23] Alam M et al. Statistical modeling of the number of deaths of children in Bangladesh. Biometrics & Biostatistics International Journal. 2014;**1**(3):00014

[24] Bereka SG, Habtewold FG. Under-five mortality of children and its determinants in Ethiopian Somali Regional State, Eastern Ethiopia. Health Science Journal. 2017;**11**(3)

[25] Getachew Y, Bekele S. Survival analysis of under-five mortality of children and its associated risk factors in Ethiopia. Journal of Biosensors and Bioelectronics. 2016;**7**(213):2

[26] Bedada D. Determinant of under-five child mortality in Ethiopia. American Journal of Statistics and Probability. 2017;**2**(2):12-18

[27] Muriithi DM, Muriithi DK. Determination of infant and child mortality in Kenya using Cox-Proportional Hazard Model. American Journal of Theoretical and Applied Statistics. 2015;**4**(5):404-413

[28] Ahmed Z, Kamal A, Kamal A. Statistical analysis of factors affecting child mortality in Pakistan. Journal of College of Physicians and Surgeons Pakistan (JCPSP). 2016;**26**(6):543

Chapter 2

Mortality Rate in Pakistan - among Low and Middle-Income Countries

Umar Bacha and Naveed Munir

Abstract

Age-specific and sex-specific cause of death determination is becoming very important task particularly for low- and middle-income countries (LMICs). Therefore, consistent openly accessible information with reproducibility may have significant role in regulating the major causes of mortality both in premature child and adults. The United Nations (UN) reported that 86% deaths (48 million deaths) out of 56 million globally deaths occurred in the LMICs in 2010. The major dilemma is that most of the deaths do not have a diagnosis of COD in such countries. Despite of the allocation of a large portion of resources to decrease the devastating impacts of chronic illnesses, their prevalence as well as the health and economic consequences remains staggeringly high. There are multiple levels of interventions that can help in bringing about significant and promising improvements in the healthcare system. Currently, Pakistan is facing double burden of malnutrition with record high prevalence rates of chronic diseases. Pakistan spends only a marginal of its GDP (1.2%) versus the recommended 5% by World Health Organization. On average, there are eight hospitals per district, with people load per hospital being 165512.452 and poor data management in the country, and we lack a consistent local registry on all-cause of mortality. This article was planned to compile the data related to major causes and disease specific mortality rates for Pakistan and link these factors to the social-economic determinants of health.

Keywords: age-specific and sex-specific, cause of death, accessible information, Pakistan, malnutrition, chronic diseases

1. Introduction

The healthcare system practiced in Pakistan is a composite of two major fields of practice, i.e., modern medicine and Unani medicine. The former one is based on practicing the evidence-based modern medicine (allopathic medicine) delivered through public sector as well as private sector healthcare facilities. The latter field of practice for therapy is traditional treatment known as *Unani* medicine (*Unani Tibb*). This system has rooted in Perso-Arabic traditional medicine or more, precisely the Greek/Greece medicine (Greek Urdu translation is *Younan or Unan or Unani*). The government of Pakistan formally recognized (through an Act passed in 1965) the Yunani medicine, along with modern medicine in 1965. Overall, Pakistan has 36,000 practitioners related to this

Provinces	Total people	Total districts	Approx. available hospitals	People load per hospital
Punjab	110,012,042	36	36 × 8 = 288	110012042/288 = 381,986.76
KPK	35,525,047	35	35 × 8 = 280	126,875.167
Sindh	47,886,051	30	30 × 8 = 240	199,525.212
Baluchistan	1,23,40000	26	26 × 8 = 208	59326.92
AJK	4045,000	10	10 × 8 = 80	50562.5
Gilgit Baltistan	883,799	14	14 × 8 = 112	7891.062
Islamabad Capital	1,164,000	1	1 × 8 = 8	145500
Total districts	211855939	160	160 × 8 = 1280	165512.452

KPK = Khyber Pakhtunkhwa; AJK = Azad Jammu & Kashmir.

Table 1.
Province-wise computed people load per tertiary care hospital in Pakistan.

branch of professionals. Another study shows around 52600 registered Unani medical practitioners in Pakistan [1]. According to WHO, about 70% or more of the population in developing countries uses traditional medicine and about 30% pharmaceutical preparations are derived from herbal medicines [2, 3].

The more vast healthcare system in Pakistan is the practice of modern medicine and hospitals, including both public and private sectors. Data from 2020 statistics show that there are almost 1282 public hospitals working throughout the country as general hospitals and specialized hospitals. Among the healthcare providers, the numbers of registered doctors, dentists, and nurses are 2,45,987; 27,360; and 1,16,659, respectively. Till the end of 2021, total numbers of districts in Pakistan are 160, which mean that there are approximately eight hospitals per district (1282/160). The total of Pakistani population as of 2020 is approximately 21,18,55,939 reported by United Nations report data that make about 2.83% of the total world population (Woldometers population report regarding Pakistan).

Table 1 represents people load per hospital calculated using the statistics tools on the basis of currently available data on the website of Pakistan Bureau of statistics, Government of Pakistan. **Table 1** explores that province Punjab has the highest patient load per hospital versus as comparative to other provinces of Pakistan. The average life expectancy of the Pakistani population is reportedly increased to 67.3 years (2019 estimate), while the population growth rate showed a decline from 2% to 1.9%. Regarding the health expenditure in Pakistan, it is shown that Pakistan spends only a marginal of its GDP (1.2%) that is below the recommendation of the World Health Organization (5%) (https://www.geo.tv/latest/354581-pakistans-health-care-system-in-2020-hospitals-doctors-increase).

2. Mortality

Identifying the gaps and evaluating factors related to mortality should be prioritized as the first step for dissecting the threshold of diseases, allocating appropriate human and monetary resources, and designing health policies. The mortality rate estimates the number of deaths in a particular time and population [4]. These rates are an indirect measure of nutritional status as well as healthcare facilities of a region. Death rates are expressed per 1000 individuals; for example, a mortality rate of 5.5 per 1000 persons means 5.5 deaths or 0.55% out of the studied population. Reports explored that in Pakistan, life expectancy in males aged 1–4 years is better (41% lower death rate), while the death rate of males aged 35–39 years is higher as compared with other low- and middle-income countries (LMICs). It was well reported that a wide range of factors might expedite the death rates, for example, natural disasters, health conditions, environmental pollution, conflicts, human-made disasters in case of deadly infections, which rapidly propagate in response to higher population density [5, 6].

2.1 Classification of mortality

Mortality is classified into various categories, such as mortality due to various chronic diseases, age, and gender, to name a few (**Table 2**). Collectively, irrespective of the cause, mortality is expressed as crude death rate (CDR). Eq. (1) is a generic formula for the determination of the crude death rate CDR.

$$\text{CDR} = \text{Overall number of death in a time point} / \text{Population under obsrvation} \times \left(10^3\right)^* \tag{1}$$

The global burden of CDR was plus seven deaths out of 1000 people per year (C.I.A., 2020). According to the World Health Organization report [7], major ten (10)

Types	Characteristics
Under 5 mortality	Under-5 mortality is also referred to as child mortality. UNICEF defines child mortality as child death that occurs between birth and age 5, while the rate is measured per 103 live births in a specific region.
Infant mortality	Infant death rate refers to the death of those under the age of 1 year
Gender-specific mortality rate	The death rate in males or females. For example, the female mortality rate is expressed as the "total number of female death ratio total number of females in a particular year." The same is the case with a male mortality rate
The mortality rate in a particular age group	Number of deaths in a particular age group ratio number of individuals living in that specific age group in a given time
Diseases specific death rate	Number of deaths allocated to a particular disease or cause ratio the total population in that area in a given time point
Maternal mortality rate	Loss of life of mothers due to the complications arising from pregnancy ratios total live births in a predefined time point.
Infant mortality rate	Loss of life among children ages less than 1-year ratio total live births in a predefined time point
Perinatal mortality rate	Also known as fetus or neonate deaths that occur intrauterine during pregnancy. Neonate deaths at 20 weeks or 28 weeks of gestation are also named stillbirths. Sometimes the stillbirths are measured in terms of fetus weight, i.e., 350 grams birth weight plus the sum of deaths among live babies who sustain life up to 7 completed days ratio total number of births in a year (C.D.C. definition)

*Mortality rate per 1,000 persons.

Table 2.
Classification of the frequently used measures of mortality.

global causes of death in the year 2019 were ischemic heart disease, stroke, pulmonary disease, respiratory infections, neonatal conditions, trachea, bronchus, lung cancers, neurological issues, diarrhea, hyperglycemia, and kidney diseases. Furthermore, World Health Organization (2016) showed around 56.9 million deaths globally due to various causes. Loss of life due to chronic disorders such as ischemic heart disease and stroke was the leading cause of 15.2 million deaths (2016) worldwide.

3. The burden associated with chronic diseases

The burden associated with chronic diseases, particularly heart-related issues, on mortality and morbidity is overwhelming. Its gravity is, however, more momentous in lower and middle-income countries probably because of relatively unstable economy and inadequate allocation of national budget for healthcare sectors. It has been reported that approximately 50% of Pakistani people face at least one of the chronic disorder [8]. The prevalence of cardiovascular diseases (CVD) in Asian countries is reportedly high in Pakistan, India, Bangladesh, Sri Lanka, and Nepal versus Chinese and Canadian subjects [9]. As of 2020, the overall death rate in Pakistan was 6.8/1,000 people, and Afghanistan was 13.89 deaths/100,000 population [10], Bangladesh 5.526/1000 person (2019). As mentioned, a wide array of factors could expedite this death rate associated with the chronic illnesses. For example, disproportionately high intake of salt and lipid consumption showed a positive association with mortality. It is, therefore, crucial to make education programs as part of the curriculum aiming to mitigate consumption of salt and *trans*-fatty acids intake as they are highly associated with the high prevalence of CVDs and hypertension in Pakistan. WHO and Food and Agriculture Organization of the United Nations strongly recommend *trans*-fat content to be less than 4% in dietary fat. The consumption of vanaspati ghee (which contains 14.2–34.3% of *trans* fat) might be a leading factor the development of cardiovascular diseases in Pakistan and other Asian countries along with many other risk factors. A significantly appreciable work on *trans*-fat reduction in food items has been done by Denmark, where the mortality due to CVD is declined by 50% over two decades [11]. Such policies need to be kept as a gold standard and amended in local contexts too.

Tobacco consumption in Pakistan is very common. It was also reported that tobacco usage is significantly associated with various types of cancers, particularly with lung cancer. It increases the risk of mortality by almost 12 times, smokers are 2–4 times more prone to develop coronary heart disorder and two times at more risk to develop stroke [12–14]. Ahmed & Colleagues [15] during a survey conducted in Pakistan reported that tobacco usage is 36% and 9% among males and females, respectively. Moreover, it was also found that out of 36% almost 15% were young adult university students [16, 17]. Therefore, efforts are needed to reduce smoking tendency for reducing the overall burden of chronic diseases and mortality rates.

At the same time, appropriate measures should be taken to motivate the public for physical activity [18], which is reportedly linked with a decrease in health related issues and mortality rates in 17 countries (Asia and Western nations) [19]. Zhou and others [20] reported that regular workout is associated with reduced risk of mortality from all causes (46%), circulatory diseases (56%), and respiratory disorders (49%). It is noted that high workout is a relatively simple and highly recommended intervention strategy for the attenuation of mortality and CVDs across all age groups [18, 21].

Population growth rate determines the availability of health facilities to general public. If the medical facilities are not increased at rates to match the growing population, morbidity and mortality rates will ultimately rise. A recent meta-analysis recommended availability and access to hospitals and surgical care in developing countries [22]. It has been suggested in literature that changing the fertility and education rate and increasing human resources in medical care [23] should be one of the focus areas to address health-related issues.

The age-standardized cancer mortality rate in Pakistan is 48600 in male and 52500 in female reported by WHO cancer country profiles (2014), the death rate due to cancer in India was 0.44 million [24], Afghanistan (2015 data) 15,211, and the United States (2015 data) 667,333 cancer-related death [10].

Pakistan's relatively high death rate (Global burden of diseases, 2010) is attributed to infections that affect the lower respiratory system, neonatal encephalopathy, and diarrheal diseases affecting all age groups and gender. However, after 1990, diarrheal diseases showed a declining trend in Pakistan; a 35% reduction was reported in 2010.

Air pollution in general and polluted in-house air from solid fuels affect the vulnerable segment of the Pakistani population. The rural–urban health disparities are also common in Pakistan. The majority of the population (60%) lives in a rural area where solid wood is burnt to generate energy. Further, poverty, accident, dietary insufficiency, sedentary lifestyle, higher carbohydrate have driven energy intake at the expense of the protein, negligible health insurance, and constrained access to hospitals are the major factors that accelerate the death rate. The actual mortality rate in Pakistan could be high as death records in the big city are maintained, but it is not usually reported in rural areas. It is, therefore, needed to consider more effective ways of registering death numbers.

Further, rural area where the majority of the population resides in Pakistan also faces a shortage of medical physicians. This scenario set the stage for an undiagnosed or unidentified cause of mortality. In conclusion, the death record, cause, and an appropriate number of medical physicians should be a national health policy priority.

4. Regional distribution of mortality rates

Figure 1 shows major causes of death in LMICs. Some of the middle-income countries work on continuously improving their healthcare services and provision. For example, Malta et al. [25] reported a significant decline in mortality (35.3%) in Brazil, demonstrating the remarkable achievement in health sector reforms in this country, particularly when deaths related to neoplasms and diabetes have been reduced. On the contrary, some economically emerging nations displayed record-high mortality rates; for instance, 6 years of data from Nigeria show 2,198 deaths in 49,287 participants who were admitted to the hospital [26] (**Figure 2**).

Abegunde et al. [27] published the burden of costs associated with chronic diseases in LMICs. The diseases burden due to chronic disorders in 23 LMICs was accountable for half (50%) of the total disease burden for the year 2005. Moreover, the death rates for men (54% higher) and women (86% higher) in 15 out of the 23 LMICs were higher versus the burden of the disease in men and women in high-income countries. Moreover, chronic diseases hardly hit women than men in the LMICs. Kassebaum et al. [28] documented that mother death ratios are 100 times more in LMICs than in developed nations, while the neonatal and fetal death rates are 10 times more than in high-income nations [29].

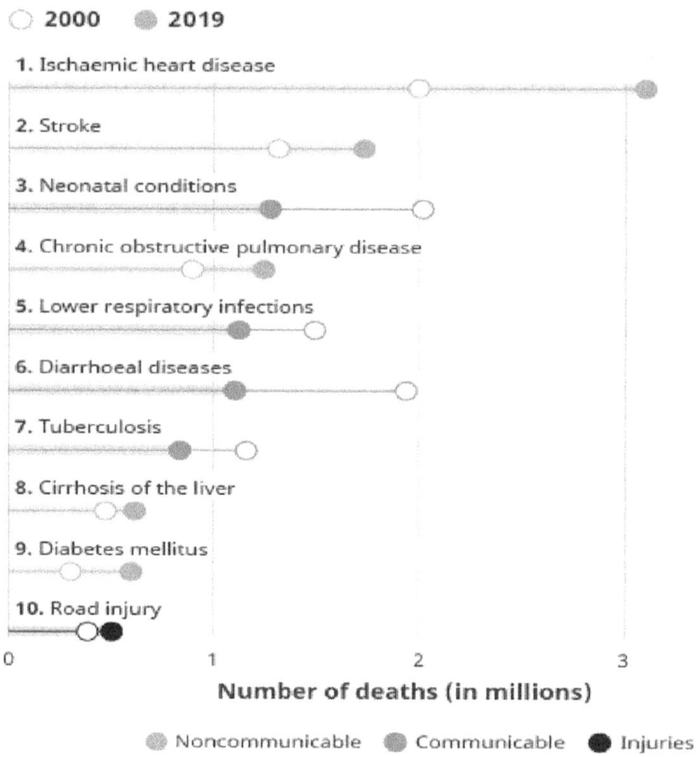

Figure 1.
Major 10 chronic disorders associated with causes of death in LMICs reported by WHO [7].

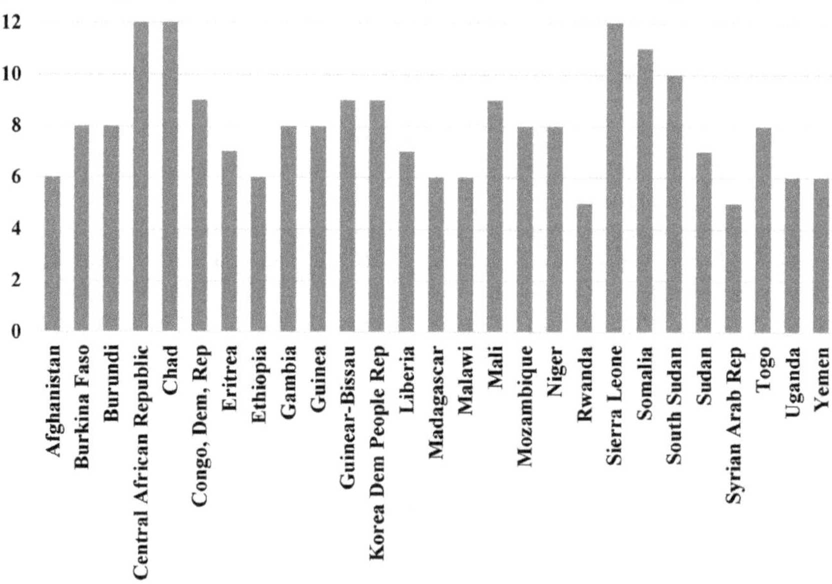

Figure 2.
Crude death rate (per 1,000 people) in lower-income countries in selected lower-income countries during the year 2019 [data generated from https://data.worldbank.org/] on 28-Nov 2021].

5. Adult mortality trend in LMICs and their comparison in Pakistan

Crude death rate/1,000 people for various middle-income countries is presented in **Figure 3**. Serbia and Bulgaria have the highest mortality rate for all age groups and genders, followed by Russian Federation and Romania. World Health Organization demographic data show a death rate of 15.4/1,000 people. Compared with neighboring nations in the European States, the death rate in Bulgaria is attributed to chronic noninfectious diseases such as cardiovascular disorders and cancer diseases. Other leading factors might be contagious diseases, malnutrition, inadequate healthcare, violence, poverty, and accidents. Other countries with undesirable ranking concerning their high death rate in the European sides were Montenegro, Kosovo, and Albania. Three countries in the Asian continent, such as Pakistan, India, and Bangladesh, occupy a similar position on the ranking.

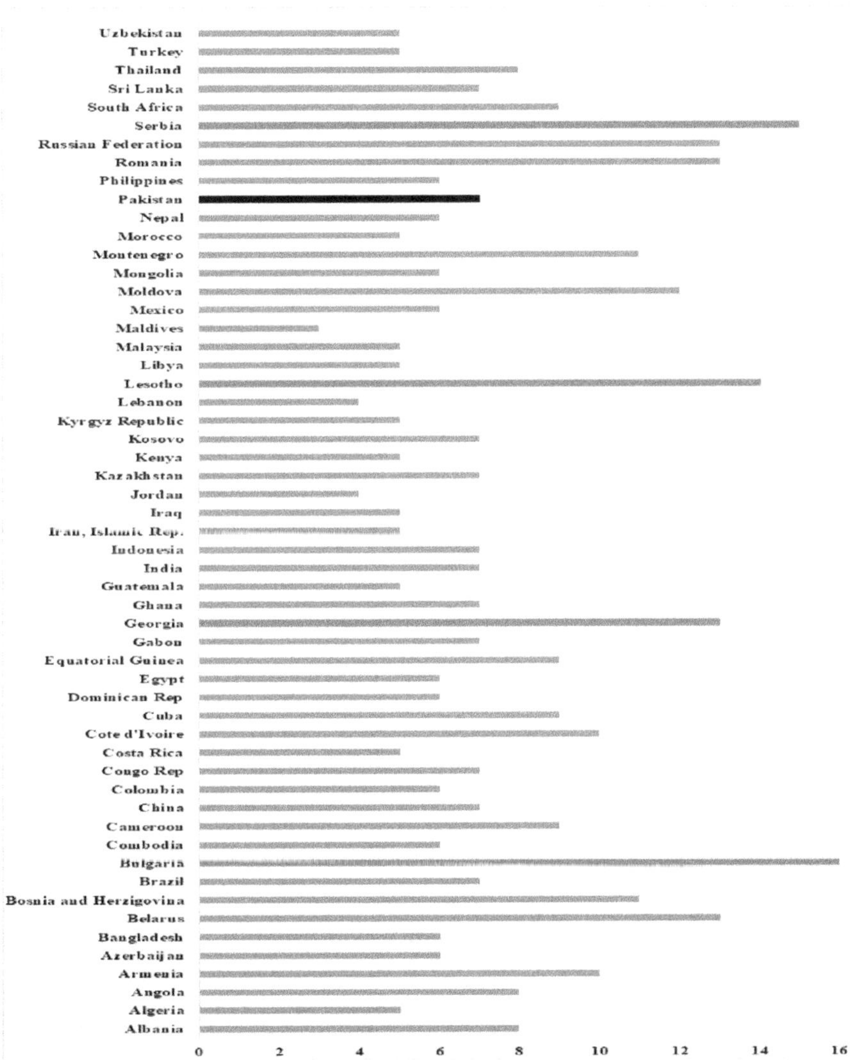

Figure 3.
Crude death rate (per 1,000 people) in LMICs and their comparison in Pakistan.

In contrast, small countries such as Malaysia, Nepal, and the Philippines where death rates were comparatively low show significant positive progress in their healthcare system.

6. Maternal mortality rate (MMR) in LMICs and their comparison in Pakistan

Bangladesh shows maternal mortality as 176/100,000 live births during 2015 [30]. Compared with other countries (India, Congo, Guatemala, Kenya, and Zambia have 456,276 births), Pakistan reported 91,076 births with MMR 319 per 100,000 live births versus the average 124/100,000 live births in the other five countries. Regarding per 1,000 live births death rate, Pakistan's performance on the ranking is not satisfactory, 49.4 compared with the average 20.4 in the other five countries. [31]. Likewise, Afghanistan has reportedly recorded high MMR at 400/100,000 live births versus other countries on this side of the world [32]. Iran's neighboring country has reduced MMR from 48/100,000 to 16/100,000 over 17 years, meaning an annual decrease of 6.3% in MMR [33]. Associated factors for high mortality may include the following: Challenges include prolonged conflicts, political instability, high blood pressure due to persistent stress, infection, bleeding, obstructed labor, unsafe abortion, dietary deficiency, low education, and poor maternal and birth in health facilities with a skilled birth attendant and newborn, postpartum care.

7. Under-5 mortality rate in LMICs and their comparison in Pakistan

The Sustainable Development Goals (SDGs) of the United Nations aim to attenuate neonatal mortality to 12 deaths/1,000 live births and under-5 mortality rates to 25 deaths/1,000 live births by 2030 [34]. African countries show a negative ranking regarding under-5 mortality 77.5 per 1000 live births and neonatal mortality 27.7 deaths/1000 live births compared with their Asian counterparts. South Asian nations present under-5 mortality as 42.1 per 1000 live births and neonatal mortality as 25.8 deaths per 1000 live births [35]. The under-5 death rate for Bangladesh was 133 in 1990, which reduced significantly to 30.2 deaths/1000 live births [36, 37], while that of Pakistan was 69.3/ 1000 live births and India 36.6 per 1000 live births [38, 39]. Baqui et al. [40] documented a comprehensive 7 years' (2007–2013) work on neonatal mortality that involved 149570 live births. The data collection was carried out from six countries, such as rural areas of Bangladesh, Ghana, India, Pakistan, the United Republic of Tanzania, and Zambia. The overall neonatal mortality in the studied countries was 30.5 /1000 live births. Overall, neonatal mortality in Pakistan from the selected population was 47.4 versus Zambia 13.6. Regarding the total mortality rate within 24 hours for the selected nation, it was 14.1 /1000 live births. The country-wise trend showed 5.1 in Zambia versus 20.1 in India. Likewise, the first 24 hours were crucial as 46.3% of all neonatal deaths followed within this time (36.2% in Pakistan compared with 65.5% in Tanzania). In parallel, in the first 6 hours mortality was less, i.e., 8.3 deaths/1000 live births for the selected countries (31.9%). Another study reported the stillbirth rate in Pakistan as 53.5/1000 births compared with the average 23.2 in India, Pakistan, the Democratic Republic of Congo, Guatemala, Kenya, Zambia [31].

Based on the data presented, it is desirable to lower neonatal mortality within the first 24 hours by adopting high standard medical care for mothers and babies before pregnancy, during, and after birth. A study from Brazil conducted (Foz do Iguassu city, from 2012 to 2016) demonstrates the high rate of neonatal mortality under the age of 5 (61%) versus average neonatal mortality in Brazil. Some of the countries showed exceptional performance in reducing neonatal mortality. For example, Bangladesh has shown remarkable improvement in attenuating the national neonatal mortality rate (1993) as 52 per 1000 live births versus 28 per 1000 live births in 2014, reflecting a 46% reduction [30]. The associated factors were a congenital fetal anomaly and low birth weight [41]. Overall, it is documented that 27.8 million neonates could lose their lives across the nation (2018–2030) due to poor neonatal and maternal care [42]. Moreover, this study associated neonatal mortality with respiratory and cardiovascular disorders (43%) and low birth weight and preterm (33%); other key factors that could accelerate neonatal deaths were placenta, cord, and pregnancy complications. Likewise, poor-quality medical and surgical conditions were lead factors. Low birth weight and preterm (42%) were the factors leading to neonatal death after discharge [42]. Kruk et al. [43] recommend universal health coverage, bringing innovation to quality healthcare that could prevent 8·6 million deaths per year. Nutrition policies such as taking care of maternal nutrition, antenatal care, and promotion of breastfeeding can prevent many of the cases of neonatal mortality.

8. Conclusion

Age-specific and sex-specific cause of death (COD) determination is becoming very important task particularly for low- and middle-income countries (LMICs). It was reported that such countries lack the proper system to record COD in such countries. Therefore, a valid policy must be adopted for assessment and reporting of up-to-date health-related data so that mitigation policies may be implemented. Currently, Pakistan is facing double burden of malnutrition in addition to the high prevalence rates of chronic diseases. There is a lack of data management in the country, and we lack a consistent local registry on all-cause of mortality. However, on reviewing the mortality rate in LMICs, it could be suggested that 1) cheap, easily accessible healthcare system should be available to all levels of the population; 2) integrating human resources for the health promotion should work together for the common goal, i.e., uplift public health; 3) most of the hospitals in rural area face huge shortage of financial resources. Timely allocation and management of resources could bring positive changes in healthcare. 4) Openly accessible data for local population should be available and 5) healthcare facilities should be centralized using modern means to update the COD nationwide.

Acknowledgements

We really appreciate the School of Health Sciences, University of Management and Technology, Lahore, Pakistan administration to give free access for downloading and compiling the reference data for the write-up of this article.

Conflict of interest

Authors have not any type of conflict of interest regarding the publication of data.

Author details

Umar Bacha* and Naveed Munir
School of Health Sciences, University of Management and Technology, Lahore, Pakistan

*Address all correspondence to: umar.bacha@umt.edu.pk

References

[1] Rahman AU. Bioprospecting of Medicinal and Food Plants: Pakistan. New York: UNDP; 2003

[2] Shaikh BT, Hatcher J. Complementary and alternative medicine in Pakistan: Prospects and limitations. Evidence-Based Complementary and Alternative Medicine. 2005;**2**(2):139-142

[3] Munir N, Mahmood Z, Yameen M, Mustafa G. Therapeutic response of Epimedium gandiflorum's different doses to restore the antioxidant potential and reproductive hormones in male albino rats. Dose-Response. 2020;**18**(3)

[4] Porta M. Mortality Rate, Morbidity Rate; Death Rate; Cumulative Death Rate; Case Fatality Rate. A Dictionary of Epidemiology. 5th ed. Oxford, UK: Oxford University Press; 2014. p. 60

[5] Bhadra A, Mukherjee A, Sarkar K. Impact of population density on Covid-19 infected and mortality rate in India. Modeling Earth Systems and Environment. 2021;**7**(1):623-629

[6] Valdés Salgado M, Smith P, Opazo MA, Huneeus N. Long-term exposure to fine and coarse particulate matter and COVID-19 incidence and mortality rate in Chile during 2020. International Journal of Environmental Research and Public Health. 2021;**18**(14):7409

[7] World Health Organization. Global health estimates: Life expectancy and leading causes of death and disability. Retrieved. 2020

[8] Jafar TH, Haaland BA, Rahman A, Razzak JA, Bilger M, Naghavi M, et al. Non-communicable diseases and injuries in Pakistan: Strategic priorities. Lancet. 2013;**381**(9885):2281-2290

[9] Quan H, Chen G, Walker R, Wielgosz A, Dai S, Tu K, et al. Incidence, cardiovascular complications and mortality of hypertension by sex and ethnicity. Heart. 2013;**99**:715-721

[10] Are C. Cancer on the global stage: Incidence and cancer-related mortality in Afghanistan. 2016.

[11] Iqbal MP. Trans fatty acids–A risk factor for cardiovascular disease. Pakistan Journal of Medical Sciences. 2014;**30**(1):194

[12] Ockene Ira S, Miller NH. Cigarette smoking, cardiovascular disease, and stroke: A statement for healthcare professionals from the American Heart Association. American Heart Association Task Force on Risk Reduction. Circulation. 1997; **96**:3243-3247

[13] U.S. Department of Health and Human Services. The Health Benefits of Smoking Cessation: A Report of the Surgeon General. Rockville, MD: U.S. Department of Health and Human Services, Centers for Disease Control, Office on Smoking and Health; 1990

[14] Fatima M, Munir N, Mahmood Z, Jahangir M. Association of Lung Cancer with Tobacco smoking; A review. National Journal of Medical and Health Sciences (NJMHS). 2020;**2**(2):97-107

[15] Ahmed R, Rizwan-ur-Rashid MP, Ahmed SW. Prevalence of cigarette smoking among young adults in Pakistan. Journal of Pakistan Medical Association. 2008;**58**(11):597-601

[16] Zaman M, Irfan U, Irshad E. Prevalence of cigarette smoking among Peshawar University students. Pakistan Journal of Chest Medicine. 2002;**8**:9-18

[17] Shaikh MA, Kamal A. Prevalence and pattern of smoking in university

students - perspective from Islamabad. Journal of College Physicians Surgery Pakistan. 2004;**14**:194

[18] Gaziano TA, Pagidipati N. Scaling up chronic disease prevention interventions in lower-and middle-income countries. Annual Review of Public Health. 2013;**34**:317-335

[19] Lear SA, Hu W, Rangarajan S, Gasevic D, Leong D, Iqbal R, et al. The effect of physical activity on mortality and cardiovascular disease in 130 000 people from 17 high-income, middle-income, and low-income countries: The PURE study. The Lancet. 2017; **390**(10113):2643-2654

[20] Zhou Y, Zhang R, Liu Y, Guo Y, Wang D, He M, et al. Association of regular physical activity with total and cause-specific mortality among middle-aged and older Chinese: A prospective cohort study. Scientific Reports. 2017;**7**(1):1-8

[21] Goenka S, Lee IM. Physical activity lowers mortality and heart disease risks. Lancet (London, England). 2017;**390**(10113):2609-2610

[22] Ng-Kamstra JS, Arya S, Greenberg SL, Kotagal M, Arsenault C, Ljungman D, et al. Perioperative mortality rates in low-income and middle-income countries: A systematic review and meta-analysis. BMJ Global Health. 2018;**3**(3):e000810

[23] Mondal MNI, Shitan M. Relative importance of demographic, socioeconomic and health factors on life expectancy in low-and lower-middle-income countries. Journal of Epidemiology. 2014;**24**(2):117-124

[24] DSouza ND, Murthy NS, Aras RY. Projection of burden of cancer mortality for India, 2011-2026. Asian Pacific Journal of Cancer Prevention. 2013;**14**(7):4387-4392

[25] Malta DC, Duncan BB, Schmidt MI, Teixeira R, Ribeiro ALP, Felisbino-Mendes MS, et al. Trends in mortality due to non-communicable diseases in the Brazilian adult population: National and subnational estimates and projections for 2030. Population Health Metrics. 2020;**18**(1):1-14

[26] Okoroiwu HU, Uchendu KI, Essien RA. Causes of morbidity and mortality among patients admitted in a tertiary hospital in southern Nigeria: A 6 year evaluation. PloS One. 2020;**15**(8):e0237313

[27] Abegunde DO, Mathers CD, Adam T, Ortegon M, Strong K. The burden and costs of chronic diseases in low-income and middle-income countries. The Lancet. 2007;**370**(9603):1929-1938

[28] Kassebaum NJ et al. Global, regional, and national levels and causes of maternal mortality during 1990-2013: A systematic analysis for the Global Burden of Disease Study 2013. Lancet. 2014;**384**(9947):980-1004

[29] Wang H et al. Global, regional, and national levels of neonatal, infant, and under-5 mortality during 1990-2013: A systematic analysis for the Global Burden of Disease Study 2013. The Lancet. 2014;**384**(9947):956

[30] Akhter H, Alam MMR. Understanding the trends of maternal and neonatal mortality in Bangladesh in the context of South Asia. Advances in Anthropology. 2019;**9**(01):56

[31] Aziz A, Saleem S, Nolen TL, Pradhan NA, McClure EM, Jessani S, et al. Why are the Pakistani maternal, fetal and newborn outcomes so poor compared to other low and middle-income countries? Reproductive Health. 2020;**17**(3):1-12

[32] Najafizada SAM, Bourgeault IL, Labonté R. Social determinants of

maternal health in Afghanistan: A review. Central Asian Journal of Global Health. 2017;**6**(1):240

[33] Mirghafourvand M, Khosravi S, Tabrizi JS, Mohammadi A, Abedi P. Two decades of Iranian midwives' activities as a health care provider under supervision in a multidisciplinary team in reducing maternal mortality. Reproductive Health. 2021;**18**(1):1-3

[34] Chao F et al. National and regional under-5 mortality rate by economic status for low-income and middle-income countries: A systematic assessment. The Lancet Global Health. 2018;**6**(5):e535-e547

[35] Unicef. U.N. inter-agency group for child mortality estimation. *Levels and trends in child mortality*. 2015.

[36] U.N. The Millennium Development Goals Report. New York: The United Nations; 2015

[37] You D et al. Global, regional, and national levels and trends in under-5 mortality between 1990 and 2015, with scenario-based projections to 2030: A systematic analysis by the U.N. Inter-agency Group for Child Mortality Estimation. 2015;**386**(10010): 2275-2286

[38] UNICEF. 2018-2021 Progress Report—Save Newborns. UNICEF South Asia, 2018.

[39] WHO. WHO|Under-five mortality. World Health Organization. 2018

[40] Baqui AH, Mitra DK, Begum N, Hurt L, Soremekun S, Edmond K, et al. Neonatal mortality within 24 hours of birth in six low-and lower-middle-income countries. Bulletin of the World Health Organization. 2016;**94**(10):752

[41] De Souza S, Duim E, Nampo FK. Determinants of neonatal mortality in the largest international border of Brazil: A case-control study. BMC Public Health. 2019;**19**(1):1-9

[42] Al-Sheyab NA, Khader YS, Shattnawi KK, Alyahya MS, Batieha A. Rate, risk factors, and causes of neonatal deaths in Jordan: Analysis of data from Jordan stillbirth and neonatal surveillance system (JSANDS). Frontiers in Public Health. 2020;**8**:1-10

[43] Kruk ME, Gage AD, Joseph NT, Danaei G, García-Saisó S, Salomon JA. Mortality due to low-quality health systems in the universal health coverage era: A systematic analysis of amenable deaths in 137 countries. The Lancet. 2018;**392**(10160):2203-2212

Section 2

Child Mortality

Chapter 3

Under-Five Mortality Causes and Prevention

Mehmet Tekin

Abstract

The under-five mortality rate (U5MR) represents children who die before reaching the age of 5 per 1000 live births. It is directly related to the development and economic income levels of countries. For this reason, high rates are observed in low- and middle-income countries (LMICs). The neonatal period deserves more attention as the decline in mortality rates has recently stalled. The most common causes of death under 5 years old are acute respiratory infections, diarrhea, malaria, and birth complications. Although neonatal disorders and birth complications have recently come to the fore, among these reasons, deaths due to infections are still high in LMICs. The crucial topics in prevention are perinatal care and vaccination. Apart from these, access to medicine, food, and clean water is essential in preventing deaths under 5. For preventive services to achieve their goal, these services must reach everyone. Ending preventable child deaths is only possible by improving access to well-equipped healthcare professionals during pregnancy and childbirth, life-saving interventions such as vaccinations, breastfeeding and the provision of low-cost medicines, and access to water and sanitation, which are now lacking in low-income countries.

Keywords: under-five mortality, neonatal mortality, low and middle-income countries, infections, perinatal mortality

1. Introduction

The under-five mortality rate (U5MR) represents children who die before reaching the age of 5 per 1000 live births [1]. The definition of live birth is a sign of life such as breathing, heartbeat, or voluntary muscular movements of the newborn after separation from the mother, regardless of the gestational age [2]. The majority of these deaths occur by preventable or treatable diseases, especially in low- and middle-income countries (LMICs). The most common causes of death under 5 years old are acute respiratory infections, diarrhea, malaria, and birth complications [3]. Underlying problems are also critical in U5MR. Malnutrition is the leading cause of about 45% of all childhood deaths [4].

The World Bank divides the world's economies into four groups according to their income status: low-income, lower-middle-income, upper-middle-income, and high-income countries. The classification is made annually based on the gross national income (GNI) per capita in US dollars (USD) of the preceding year. According to the current data for 2021, countries with a GNI per capita of less than 1046 USD are classified as low-income countries, and those with less than 12,695 USD are classified as middle-income countries [5].

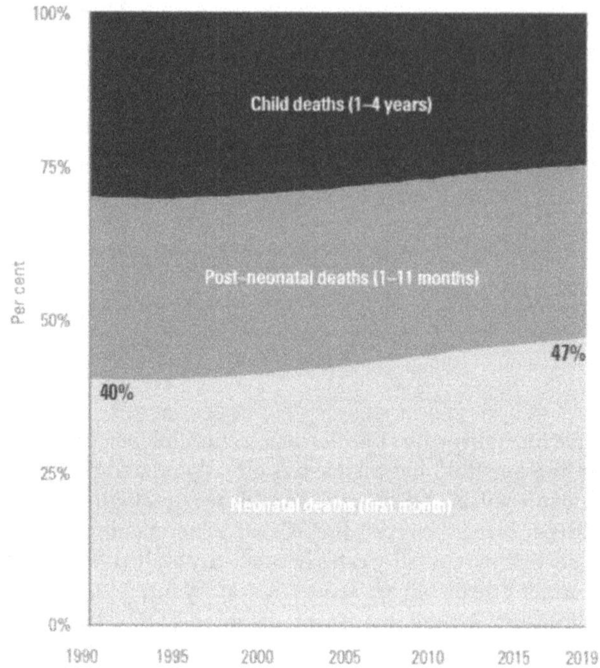

Figure 1.
Distribution of global under-five deaths by age, 1990–2019 [7].

Child mortality under the age of 5 consists of several subgroups. These are neonatal mortality (birth—the first month of life), infant mortality (birth—the first year of life), and child mortality (1–5 years). Looking at the U5MR in each subgroup, it is observed that the neonatal group has the highest risk. Among this population, the youngest has the highest mortality rate. A review showed that approximately one-third of all neonatal deaths occur within the first day after birth, and nearly three-fourths occur within the first week of life [6].

Data from the last three decades show that the fastest decline in U5MR occurred between 2000 and 2009. Globally, the annual rate of reduction (ARR) was 1.9 percent in 1990–1999, 4.0 percent in 2000–2009, and 3.4 percent in 2010–2019. While 1 out of every 11 children could not see their 5th birthday in the 1990s, this number dropped to 1 in 27 in 2019. In 34 LMICs, U5MR was reduced by more than two-thirds between 1990 and 2019 [7].

Although there was a similar decrease in neonatal mortality rates (NMR), it was slower than the decline in child mortality rates between 1 and 59 months. Between 1990 and 2019, the average ARR for child mortality in the first 1–59 months was 3.6 percent, compared to only 2.5 percent in the neonatal period. As a result of these rates, deaths in children under 5 years of age began to concentrate in the neonatal period. While the ratio of newborn deaths to all childhood deaths under 5 was 40 percent in 1990, this rate increased to 47 percent in 2019 (**Figure 1**) [7].

The U5MR is a good indicator of the healthcare system and general social-economic development. The reasons are as follows:

- First, these data precede results, not inputs. For example, the number of doctors and nurses per child is an input, it is related to child health, but positive/negative inputs do not necessarily mean that outcomes will be positive/negative. The U5MR clearly shows the extent to which these inputs achieve their goal.

- The U5MR is closely related to some negative socio-economic factors (malnutrition, low immunization rates, poor maternal health, and education). Therefore, it is a strong indicator of inequality and systemic health problems.

- At the same time, as many of these deaths are preventable, the rate reflects better than any other measure the lack of access to critical and essential quality health care, including family planning, antenatal and postnatal services, and disease prevention and case management.

For these and similar reasons, many global initiatives, mainly the United Nations Global Strategy for Women's Children's and Adolescents' Health (2016–2030) [8] and the Sustainable Development Goals (SDG) [9], have set child survival goals to improve the U5MR.

In this chapter, we aim to examine the causes of death under the age of 5 and the methods of prevention.

2. Causes

In LMICs, maternal and neonatal diseases, respiratory infections and tuberculosis, enteric and other infections, and malaria are the leading causes of under-five mortality. While in high-income countries, complex neonatal conditions such as prematurity top the list of causes of under-five mortality, in LMICs, infectious diseases still rank high among causes of death.

2.1 Maternal and neonatal disease

Since the decline in NMR has not been achieved to a similar extent as in U5MR, the rate of deaths due to maternal and neonatal diseases among under-five mortality has increased recently, especially in high-income countries. In one study, the two most common causes of death in the neonatal period in LMICs were perinatal asphyxia and severe infections such as sepsis, meningitis, and pneumonia [10]. Approximately 23% of the 2.5 million annual infant deaths in the neonatal period are related to infections [7]. Deaths are due to complications associated with prematurity account for about one-fifth of neonatal deaths in these countries. These three causes account for 90% of total neonatal deaths in LMICs [11].

2.2 Respiratory infections and tuberculosis

Despite improvements in living conditions and increases in vaccination rates, respiratory infections are the leading cause of under-five death after neonatal diseases in LMICs. It is estimated that approximately 100 million pneumonia episodes occur annually under 5 [12]. With the increase in Pneumococcal conjugate and Haemophilus influenza type b vaccination, changes in the etiology of pneumonia have occurred recently. Among bacterial pathogens, non-type b Haemophilus influenza and Staphylococcus aureus are more common, whereas RSV stands out among viral pathogens. Although less common, CMV pneumonia can be fatal in HIV-infected and immunosuppressed patients [12].

Within this group of diseases, tuberculosis occupies a special place in LMICs. About a quarter of the world's population is infected with Mycobacterium tuberculosis, which is not always easy to treat with its extrapulmonary involvement and resistant strains [13]. About half of all people with tuberculosis live in eight countries: Bangladesh, China, India, Indonesia, Nigeria, Pakistan, Philippines, and

South Africa [14]. In 2019, there were a total of 50,000 deaths due to tuberculosis in children under 5 years of age [15].

2.3 Enteric infections

Enteral infections are the leading cause of death in children under 5 years among all infections, causing 1.5–2 million deaths per year [16, 17]. In LMICs, there are six episodes of diarrhea per year in infants and three episodes per year in children [18]. Rotavirus, Cryptosporidium, Shigella, and enterotoxigenic Escherichia coli (ETEC) are the most common pathogens observed in the moderate and severe diarrheal disease under 5 years of age in LMICs [19]. In the past, severe dehydration and fluid loss were the main causes of death from diarrhea. Other causes, such as septic bacterial infections, are now increasingly responsible for all diarrheal deaths [20].

2.4 Malaria

Infection with Plasmodium falciparum potentially is fatal and most commonly manifests as a nonspecific febrile illness often without localizing signs. About 635,000 deaths from malaria occurred in LMICs in 2019, of which more than 50% were children under 5 years of age [14]. Moreover, malaria in pregnancy leads to fetal growth retardation, low birth weight, and later malaria infection in the infant, which increases neonatal mortality [21, 22]. In sub-Saharan Africa, a region at high risk of malaria, peripheral malaria is detected in the blood of about half of pregnant women during antenatal care [23].

In addition to these main causes, some factors increase the frequency and treatability or mortality of these diseases. The Covid-19 pandemic, which has been ongoing for about two years, has placed a heavy burden on the health care system. A survey by UNICEF conducted in 77 countries shows that almost 68 percent of countries reported slight reductions in health checks and immunizations for children. In addition, 63 percent of countries reported interruptions in antenatal checkups and 59 percent in postnatal care [24]. In regions with a high burden of HIV, malaria, and tuberculosis, the Covid-19 pandemic may increase HIV-related deaths by 10%, tuberculosis-related deaths by 20%, and malaria-related deaths by up to 36% over 5 years [7].

Some other exacerbating underlying factors include food insecurity, inadequate feeding practices, household air pollution, lack of hygiene, and access to safe water or adequate sanitation.

3. Trends in under-five mortality

While the U5MR was about 85 per 1000 live births worldwide in 1990, it dropped to 38 per 1000 live births by 2019, a decline of over 50%. According to 2019 data, the global NMR was 17 per 1000 live births. While this rate was 11 per 1000 for children aged 1 month to 1 year, it was 10 per 1000 for children aged 1–5 years. The gap between the highest and lowest regional U5MR narrowed from 171 deaths per 1000 live births in 1990 to 73 in 2019. In 1990, the number of countries with a mortality rate above 100 per 1000 live births was over 50, while this number has dropped to 5 in 2019. Variation in NMR and U5MR in LMICs by year is shown in **Figures 2–5**.

Despite these developments, U5MR in low-income countries remains high. These countries are all located in sub-Saharan Africa. In sub-Saharan Africa, the region with the highest U5MR, one in 13 children does not reach the age of five. This rate is

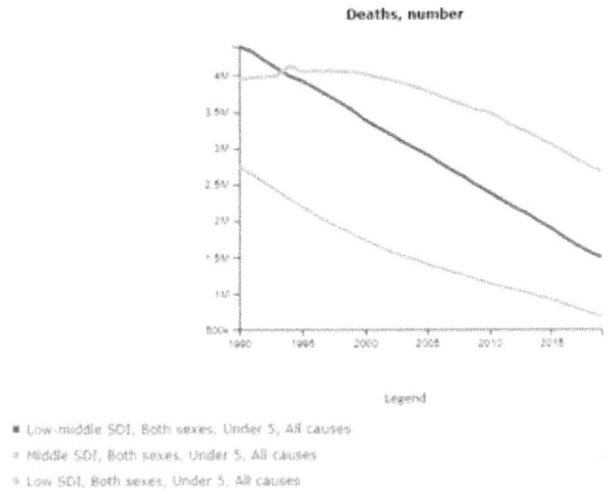

Figure 2.
Number of under-5 deaths between 1990 and 2019. Data were obtained from the healthdata.org website.

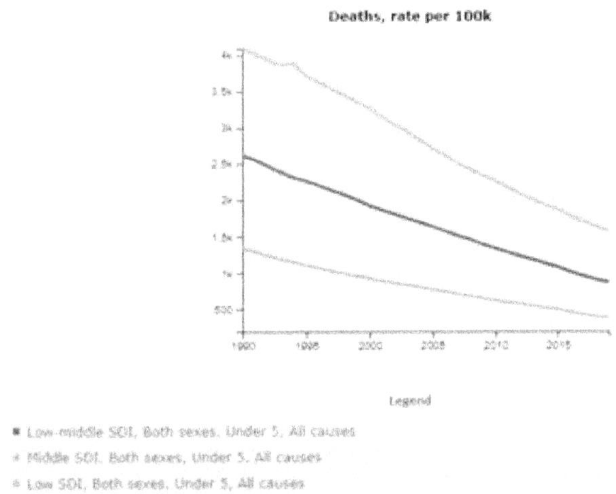

Figure 3.
U5MR between 1990 and 2019. Data were obtained from the healthdata.org website.

15–20 times higher than in developed countries. Of the 37 countries in this region, 31 have a high mortality rate (U5MR above 50 per 1000 live births). Although sub-Saharan Africa and Central and South Asia account for about 50% of children under 5, 80% of all under 5 deaths in 2019. On a country basis, nearly half of under-five deaths in 2019 occurred in five countries: Nigeria, India, Pakistan, the Democratic Republic of the Congo and, Ethiopia. Nigeria and India alone account for nearly a third. The alteration of mortality rates by regions over time is shown in **Figure 6**.

When evaluating neonatal mortality, sub-Saharan Africa has the highest rate in 2019 (27 per 1000), followed by Central and South Asia (24 per 1000). Nearly 80% of neonatal deaths in 2019 occurred in these two regions. From 1990 to 2019, sub-Saharan Africa was the only SDG region without a decline in neonatal mortality due to the relatively low decrease in NMR and increase in the birth rate. In this period, newborn deaths did not decline in 21 of 48 countries in sub-Saharan Africa, and the total number of newborn deaths remained stable at about 1 million per year.

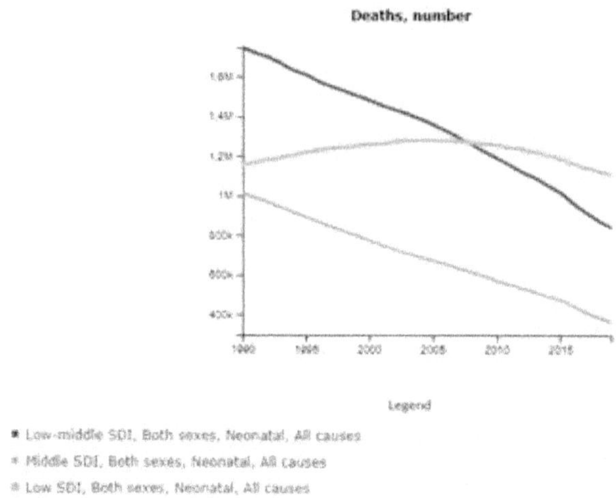

Figure 4.
Number of neonatal deaths between 1990 and 2019. Data were obtained from the healthdata.org website.

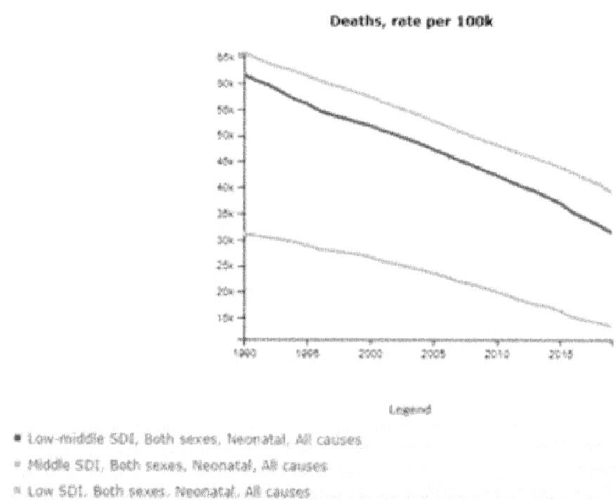

Figure 5.
NMR between 1990 and 2019. Data were obtained from the healthdata.org website.

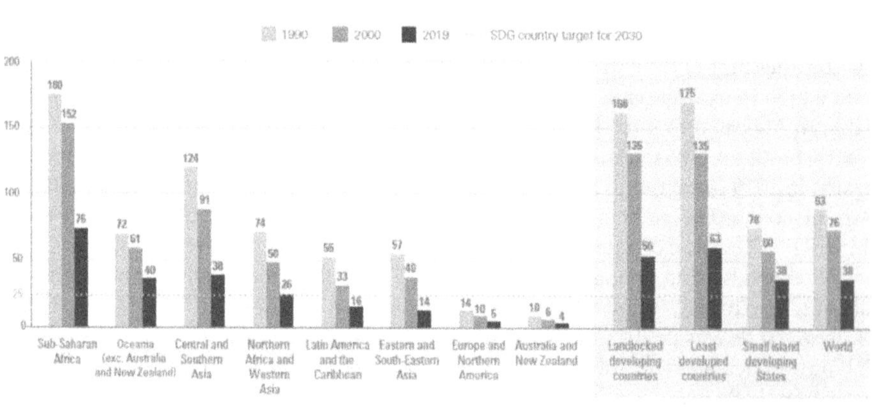

Figure 6.
U5MR (deaths per 1000 live births) by regions, 1990, 2000, and 2019 [7].

The difference between the sexes has tended to narrow over time in under-five mortality. In general, the risk of death is higher for boys under the age of 5 than for girls. However, due to regional risks, the mortality rate of girls is much higher than expected in some countries. These countries are located in the South and West Asia. After 1990, there were similar developments in this area, and the number of countries with higher than expected girl mortality dropped from 25 to 7.

The SDG aims to finish under-five mortality from preventable causes by reducing the NMR to 12 and below per 1000 live births and the U5MR to 25 and below per 1000 live births by 2030. If the current trend in under-five mortality continues, 27 percent of the 195 countries evaluated in the latest UNICEF report will not meet the SDG target. Achieving the 2030 target requires high-level efforts and a focus on child mortality in the remaining 53 countries. All these countries are in the status of LMICs. In light of current data, it is estimated that 48 million children under the age of 5 will die between 2020 and 2030. Nearly 80% of these deaths are expected to occur in sub-Saharan Africa and Central and South Asia, where almost all of the countries they host are LMICs. Moreover, if current trends continue, it does not seem possible for nearly 90% of sub-Saharan African countries to reach the neonatal mortality target of the SDG [7].

4. Prevention

Access to life-saving interventions is at the forefront of consistently reducing mortality in LMICs. Examining the main causes of under-five deaths in these countries, it is observed that care during and after birth, vaccinations, and preventive and therapeutic services in early childhood play a crucial role [25]. An analysis conducted in 118 LMICs found that disrupting access to basic life-saving interventions could cause millions of under-five deaths in as little as six months [26]. We can consider protective interventions under several headings:

4.1 Perinatal care

Due to the increase in the birth rate and the dependence of mother-infant life on basic life-saving interventions, prenatal, natal and postnatal care is a priority issue in LMICs. At this point, comprehensive prenatal care, skilled and rapid care during childbirth, regular postnatal care for mother and child, and high-quality and adequate care for premature and sick newborns should be the goal. For reasons other than congenital anomalies causing one in 10 neonatal deaths [27], the following precautions should be taken:

Home visits during pregnancy can play an active role in reducing NMR. A large-scale study in India has shown that antenatal care provided by Accredited Social Health Activists significantly reduces infant mortality rates under 1-year-old [28]. All pregnant women should be visited by experienced teams at least four times during pregnancy, including one visit in the first trimester. At these visits, preeclampsia and eclampsia can be diagnosed and treatment initiated in appropriate cases. In addition, these visits provide an opportunity to start folic acid and iron supplements that improve fetal health and to test for HIV, which is at risk of transmission from mother to fetus. Home visits can also help ensure that adequate precautions are taken in areas where malaria is common. Tetanus vaccinations recommended during pregnancy can be given during these visits. Finally, these visits can encourage pregnant women to deliver in the hospital and provide information about birth complications and nutrition.

Facility-based delivery should be provided to all pregnant women and, expectant mothers should be encouraged in this regard. Basic hygiene rules such as hand washing, sterile cord-cutting, and cord care should be followed in these facilities. To achieve this, using clean delivery kits (CDK) should be expanded for both home and facility deliveries. The use of CDK containing soap, gloves, cord ties, and other sterile equipment has been shown to reduce neonatal mortality and neonatal tetanus in studies in LMIC countries [29–31]. Drugs (oxytocin, etc.) and materials (partograph, etc.) used in the active management of labor should also be available. In communities where access to facilities is not possible, the number of staff with basic emergency obstetric and newborn care (BEmONC) training should be increased. However, a fast and safe referral and transport system should be ready in case of complications where the capabilities and knowledge of these staff may be inadequate. The purpose of this transportation is to transport the patient to facilities where comprehensive emergency obstetric and newborn care (CEmONC) can be provided.

In the postnatal period, attention should be paid to hypothermia and allow the mother to feed her baby within the first hour of life. It should be ensured that the mother and newborn stay in the facility for the first 24 hours, and an early postnatal visit should be scheduled to recognize the danger signs. In cases of suspected or proven infection, neonates should be treated with antibiotics, and newborns at risk should be followed up in neonatal intensive care units with adequate personnel and equipment.

4.2 Vaccination and medication

Vaccination is an essential component of primary health care and an indisputable human right. Also, it is the single most effective prevention method for reducing mortality in children under 5. The following vaccines are at the forefront of preventing early childhood deaths: measles, polio, diphtheria, tetanus and pertussis, Haemophilus influenza type B, pneumococcal, and rotavirus vaccines. Reaching large populations with effective community health programs is crucial for vaccination success. Despite significant advances in immunization, too many children worldwide—including around 20 million infants each year—do not have adequate access to vaccines [32].

Since it is more difficult to diagnose tuberculosis (TB) in childhood, prevention may be more feasible than cure. At this point, neonatal use of the BCG vaccine, which is still the only vaccine against tuberculosis, could be the solution. Neonatal administration of BCG has been associated with a lower prevalence of TB disease [33].

Access to antibiotics and antimalarial to treat diarrhea, malaria, and lower respiratory tract infections also contribute to reducing child mortality. In diarrhea, oral rehydration solution and zinc supplementation help reduce mortality.

4.3 Community-based prevention

Community health workers play a vital role in providing health care to underprivileged communities. Public health workers organize public education programs, especially in the field of preventive health services. The performance of these workers is critical to increasing vaccination and breastfeeding rates, disseminating malaria prophylaxis devices such as insecticide-treated bed nets, and improving hygiene behaviors.

Studies in rural areas of three LMICs found that proximity to health facilities was a significant risk factor for infant, child, and general under-five mortality [34–36]. Similarly, a meta-analysis found that a distance of over 5 km from the health facility can increase mortality by up to 60% in newborns and children under five years of age [37]. In these and similar situations, governments should eliminate inequality of opportunity among communities and ensure access to health services for all. For example, maternity waiting homes, initiated under the leadership of the World Health Organization (WHO), can be expanded for pregnant women with limited access to facilities.

The integrated management of childhood diseases, in collaboration with national and international organizations, will help to address regional and cross-national disparities and share experience and knowledge. Finally, it is essential to build a people-centered and high-quality health system to implement all these preventive measures. At the same time, families' desire for medical care and behavior to seek medical help when their children are ill should be encouraged.

4.4 Nutrition education and management of malnutrition

Encouraging breastfeeding is a practical and cost-effective method of preventing early childhood deaths. However, about two out of three infants do not have access to exclusive breastfeeding for 6 months. Breast milk provides all the energy and nutrients a baby needs in the first months of life, and continues to meet at least one-third of the baby's nutritional needs during the second half of the first year [38]. Breastfeeding not only improves the child's nutrition but also protects the child from the dirty water used in food preparation and cleaning kitchen utensils. Vitamin A supplementation should be encouraged as it has been proven to reduce the risk of illness and death from measles and diarrhea. Access to clean water and ensuring hygiene will be particularly effective in reducing the incidence of diarrheal diseases. Screening for acute malnutrition allows early detection of cases with a risk for mortality.

5. Conclusion

The U5MR has been significantly reduced over the last 30 years through concerted action and resource allocation. The next goal of countries achieving the SDG targets should be to ensure the protection of children by eliminating inequalities that arise for reasons such as household income, race and ethnicity, and subnational division. While there are some developments in child health globally, 75% of countries failing to meet the SDG targets are found in sub-Saharan Africa clearly showing the inequality that children face in terms of their chances of survival due to birthplace. These inequalities are exacerbated in times of crisis, such as the Covid-19 pandemic, and have an even more negative impact on vulnerable children [39]. Attention should be given to sub-Saharan Africa, where mortality rates are highest in all age groups and the population continues to grow, considering that 11 million children could be saved by 2030 if all countries achieve the SDG targets.

On the other hand, newborns, whose mortality rate is declining more slowly than other age groups and therefore continues to increase their share in the under-five mortality rate, also deserve special attention. Moreover, it is more difficult to reduce the number of deaths during this period due to the establishment of more advanced health care facilities and the need for quality health care services over a longer time, beginning with the antenatal period. In addition to these, it is necessary to provide adequate health services during childbirth and in the early postnatal period. These services, along with NMR, will also reduce maternal mortality rates, the risk of stillbirths, and disability.

When we look at under-five deaths as a whole, it is essential that evidence-based life-saving interventions are accessible and accepted in the community. In addition, the impact of contextual factors such as female empowerment, nutrition, and health system resources should not be ignored in achieving success.

Another issue that should not be ignored in child mortality is the reliability of the data. In resource-poor areas, deaths may not be reported, or the cause of death may not be identified. This information may not be made available to national authorities and international health organizations promptly. Therefore, there is a need for a high-level integrated database at local, national, regional, and global levels, especially for under-five mortality data.

In summary, ending preventable child deaths is only possible by improving access to well-equipped health care professionals during pregnancy and childbirth, life-saving interventions such as vaccinations, breastfeeding, and the provision of low-cost medicines, and access to water and sanitation, which are now lacking in low-income countries.

Author details

Mehmet Tekin
Faculty of Medicine, Department of Pediatrics, Baskent University, Konya, Turkey

*Address all correspondence to: dr.mehmettekin@gmail.com

References

[1] Black RE, Laxminarayan R, Temmerman M, et al. Reproductive, Maternal, Newborn, and Child Health: Disease Control Priorities. Third ed. Vol. 2. Washington (DC): The International Bank for Reconstruction and Development / The World Bank; 2016 Chapter 1

[2] Sullivan, J. and N. K. Tureeva. INFANT AND CHILD MORTALITY. Uzbekistan Health Examination Survey 2002. Calverton, Maryland, USA: Analytical and Information Center, State Department of Statistics, and ORC Macro; 2004

[3] GBD 2017 Causes of Death Collaborators. Global, regional, and national age-sex-specific mortality for 282 causes of death in 195 countries and territories, 1980-2017: a systematic analysis for the Global Burden of Disease Study 2017. Lancet. 2018;**392**(10159):1736-1788

[4] United Nations Children's Fund (UNICEF) and the World Health Organization (WHO). Countdown to 2030: Tracking Progress towards Universal Coverage for Reproductive, Newborn and Child Health: The 2017 Report. Washington, DC: UNICEF and WHO; 2017

[5] https://blogs.worldbank.org/opendata/new-world-bank-country-classifications-income-level-2021-2022

[6] Jeeva SM et al. When Do Newborns Die? A systematic review of timing of overall and cause-specific neonatal deaths in developing countries. Journal of Perinatology. 2016;**36**(1):1-11

[7] United Nations Inter-agency Group for Child Mortality Estimation (UN IGME). Levels & Trends in Child Mortality: Report 2019, Estimates Developed by the United Nations Inter-agency Group for Child Mortality Estimation. New York, NY: United Nations Children's Fund; 2019

[8] https://www.everywomaneverychild.org/wp-content/uploads/2017/10/EWEC_GSUpdate_Full_EN_2017_web-1.pdf

[9] http://sustainabledevelopment.un.org/

[10] Usman F, Imam A, Farouk ZL, Dayyabu AL. Newborn mortality in sub-Saharan Africa: Why is perinatal asphyxia still a major cause? Annals of Global Health. 2019;**85**:112

[11] Alliance for Maternal and Newborn Health Improvement (AMANHI) mortality study group. Population-based rates, timing, and causes of maternal deaths, stillbirths, and neonatal deaths in south Asia and sub-Saharan Africa: A multi-country prospective cohort study. The Lancet Global Health. 2018;**6**(12):1297-1308

[12] Marangu D, Zar HJ. Childhood pneumonia in low-and-middle-income countries: An update. Paediatric Respiratory Reviews. 2019;**32**:3-9

[13] Global tuberculosis report 2020. Geneva: World Health Organization; 2020.

[14] https://www.who.int/health-topics/tuberculosis

[15] http://ghdx.healthdata.org/gbd-results-tool

[16] Bryce J, Boschi-Pinto C, Shibuya K, Black RE, WHO Child Health Epidemiology Reference Group. WHO estimates of the causes of death in children. Lancet. 2005;**365**(9465):1147-1152

[17] Boschi-Pinto C, Velebit L, Shibuya K. Estimating child mortality due to diarrhoea in developing

countries. Bulletin of the World Health Organization. 2008;**86**(9):710-717

[18] Kosek M, Bern C, Guerrant RL. The global burden of diarrhoeal disease, as estimated from studies published between 1992 and 2000. Bulletin of the World Health Organization. 2003;**81**(3):197-204

[19] Kotloff KL, Nataro JP, Blackwelder WC, et al. Burden and aetiology of diarrhoeal disease in infants and young children in developing countries (the Global Enteric Multicenter Study, GEMS): a prospective, case-control study. Lancet. 2013;**382**(9888):209-222

[20] https://www.who.int/health-topics/breastfeeding

[21] Guyatt HL, Snow RW. Impact of malaria during pregnancy on low birth weight in sub-Saharan Africa. Clinical Microbiology Reviews. 2004;**17**(4): 760-769

[22] Le Port A, Cottrell G, Martin-Prevel Y, et al. First malaria infections in a cohort of infants in Benin: biological, environmental and genetic determinants. Description of the study site, population methods and preliminary results. BMJ Open. 2012;**2**(2):e000342

[23] Bauserman M, Conroy AL, North K, et al. An overview of malaria in pregnancy. Seminars in Perinatology. 2019;**43**(5):282-290

[24] https://data.unicef.org/resources/levels-and-trends-in-child-mortality/

[25] MCEE-WHO methods and data sources for child causes of death 2000-2017. Geneva: World Health Organization; 2018

[26] Roberton T et al. Early estimates of the indirect effects of the COVID- 19 pandemic on maternal and child mortality in low-income and middle- income countries: A modelling study. The Lancet Global Health. July 2020;**8**:E901-E908

[27] https://www.who.int/news-room/fact-sheets/detail/congenital-anomalies

[28] Nadella P, Subramanian SV, Roman-Urrestarazu A. The impact of community health workers on antenatal and infant health in India: A cross-sectional study. SSM-Population Health. 2021;**15**:100872

[29] Park JH, Hamer DH, Mbewe R, et al. Components of clean delivery kits and newborn mortality in the Zambia Chlorhexidine Application Trial (ZamCAT): An observational study. PLoS Medicine. 2021;**18**(5):e1003610

[30] Raza SA, Avan BI. Disposable clean delivery kits and prevention of neonatal tetanus in the presence of skilled birth attendants. International Journal of Gynaecology and Obstetrics. 2013; **120**(2):148-151

[31] Seward N, Osrin D, Li L, Costello A, Pulkki-Brannstrom AM, Houweling TAJ, et al. Association between clean delivery kit use, clean delivery practices, and neonatal survival: Pooled analysis of data from three sites in South Asia. PLoS Medicine. 2012;**9**(2):e1001180

[32] https://www.who.int/health-topics/vaccines-and-immunization

[33] Mangtani P, Abubakar I, Ariti C, et al. Protection by BCG vaccine against tuberculosis: A systematic review of randomized controlled trials. Clinical Infectious Diseases. 2014;**58**:470-480

[34] Schoeps A, Gabrysch S, Niamba L, et al. The effect of distance to health-care facilities on childhood mortality in rural Burkina Faso. American Journal of Epidemiology. 2011;**173**(5):492-498

[35] Okwaraji YB, Edmond KM. Proximity to health services and child

survival in low- and middle-income countries: A systematic review and meta-analysis. BMJ Open. 2012;**2** (e001196):1-9

[36] Karra M, Fink G, Canning D. Facility distance and child mortality: A multicountry study of health facility access, service utilization, and child health outcomes. International Journal of Epidemiology. 2017;**46**(3):817-826

[37] Rojas-Gualdrón D, Caicedo-Velázquez B. Distance from healthcare facilities and early life mortality: A systematic review and meta-analysis. Revista Facultad Nacional de Salud Pública. 2017;**35**(3):420-431

[38] https://www.who.int/health-topics/diarrhoea

[39] https://www.oecd.org/coronavirus/policy-responses/covid-19-crises-and-fragility/

Section 3

Stress Reduction Therapy

Chapter 4

Music and Music Therapy Is a Medicine for Stress

Gayatri Devi Ramalingam, G. Sridevi, Jothi Priya Amirtham, Preetha Santhakumar and S. Saravanakumar

Abstract

Stress is a feeling of emotional or physical tension. It can be triggered by any event or thought that causes you to feel dissatisfied, angry, or anxious. The body's response to a challenge or demand is known as stress. The importance of developing cost-effective stress reduction interventions is high due to the difficulty of reducing or preventing stress without professional help and the large demand for non-pharmacological stress reduction interventions. Music therapy is the clinical application of musical therapies to improve a client's quality of life based on scientific evidence. Music therapists use both active and receptive music experiences to help clients improve their health in cognitive, motor, emotional, communicative, social, sensory, and educational domains by using music and its many facets, which include physical, emotional, mental, social, aesthetic, and spiritual domains. Nowadays, stress is increasingly widespread among all individuals all over the world, and people are more aware of it than ever before. This chapter may assist the general public in gaining a broad understanding of the role of music therapy in stress management, as well as assisting individuals in self-recovery.

Keywords: music, stress, therapy, brain, neurotransmitters

1. Introduction

"Stress" is a term used to describe the impacts of anything that disrupts physiological equilibrium. The "stressor" is the actual threat to an organism, and the "stress response" is the organism's response to the stressor. *Selye* recognised that strong, sustained stress reactions could lead to tissue damage and disease, despite the fact that stress responses evolved as adaptive mechanisms [1]. The two types of stress are acute and chronic. Acute stress lasts for a few days or weeks, whereas chronic stress lasts for weeks or months. At the time of stress, the autonomic nervous system gets activated to protect the body from it. When instant fight-or-flight is possible, autonomic and hormonal activities accelerate, maximising the opportunities for physical exertion [2]. There are two important types of stereotypy. Individual variances in stress reactions to the same scenario exist, despite the fact that different conditions tend to evoke diverse patterns of stress responses. The term "response stereotypy" refers to the tendency to demonstrate a consistent pattern of stress responses across a variety of stressors. Situational stereotypy refers to the degree to which distinct contexts stimulate diverse patterns of physiological response [3]. Some people exhibit stress responses linked with active coping in a

IntechOpen

range of contexts, whereas others exhibit stress responses more associated with unconcerned attention.

Humans are particularly susceptible to the negative consequences of chronic stressors, presumably because of their strong ability for symbolic cognition, which can evoke persistent stress reactions to a wide range of stressful living and working environments. Psychosocial stressors and chronic disease have a complicated interaction. Anxiety and mood disorders, aggressive dyscontrol issues, hypo-immune dysfunction, medical morbidity, structural alterations in the CNS, and early death are all linked to exposure to strong and chronic stressors during childhood [4]. Acute stress disorder (ASD) and post-traumatic stress disorder (PTSD) are the two most common trauma disorders. Injury, property damage, loss of finances, grief, and a perceived stress threat are all factors linked to the development of PTSD and mental health disorders [5]. A traumatic incident involving actual or threatened death or significant harm, and symptom clusters including re-experience of the traumatic event are common elements of both of these diseases [6]. Other stress-related repercussions have been documented, including a rise in smoking habit, substance abuse, crashes, insomnia, and anorexia. People who live in more stressful circumstances such as populations with greater divorce rates, business failures, major hazards smoke more and have a higher lung cancer and COPD incidence [7]. Stress from life events and chronically stressful environments have also been connected to increased alcohol use. There is additional evidence that the relationship between personality and environmental adversity is bidirectional. Following the perception of an acute stressful event, changes in the neurological, circulatory, endocrine, and immunological systems occur. These changes are a normal feature of the stress response, and they are generally adaptive, at least in the short term [8].

2. Music interference

Music interventions can be defined as intentional music activities if they engage hearing to pre-taped music provided by clinician or healthcare professionals, if the involvement is self-administered by the person or if the intervention involves music creating or singing without the involvement of a professional musician or a therapeutic context. Specific aspects of music are thought to have an impact on the stress-relieving benefits of music therapies. Song lyric composition, interpretation of selected song lyrics, and identification of song names or lyrics that depict stresses and coping mechanisms are all examples of music therapy techniques for linguistic self-expression. One of the most important modifiers of music-related excitation and relaxation is the pace of the song. Music with a slow tempo (60–80 beats per minute), such as meditation music, has been linked to lower heart rates and increased calm [9]. When instrumental music is used instead of music with lyrics, the effects of music treatments on stress reduction are generally larger [10]. According to several studies, music with lyrics is more provocative and stimulating than calming. Through the possible calming effects, the use of music with lyrics may increase the good benefits of music therapies on stress reduction. Furthermore, some research compared the stress responses of people who listened to live music vs. those who listened to pre-recorded music, with live music showing to be the most stress-relieving [11, 12]. Several studies have found that listening to music has a favourable impact on stress-related outcomes. Listening to relaxing music before, during, and after medical operations has been linked to decreased cortisol levels, which has been linked to a reduction in tension and/or anxiety in medical settings [12–15]. Background music had a considerable impact on behavioural expressions of tension in specific parts of the body, as well as pain-related verbalizations.

Patients' verbal comments of music's usefulness in promoting relaxation were backed up by the behavioural measure. Other stress-reduction studies could benefit from behavioural observations of tension, and they could be used as a credible dependent measure [16].

3. Music therapy or music-relaxed therapy

Music is a vital component in improving one's ability to express oneself, reducing anxiety, treating physiological disorders, effectively managing time, learning coping techniques, and overall life quality. Music therapy (MT) is a goal-oriented and purposeful practise in which therapists use musical expression and the memories, emotions, and experiences it evokes to work with individuals or groups. MT is one of the oldest treatment techniques, and it has been used to treat diseases in various cultures. Music elements such as rhythm, melody, and harmony are used therapeutically in MT. Active and receptive music therapy are the two primary forms of music therapy. Playing simple instruments, dancing, or singings are common forms of active music therapy. This type of exercise promotes physical stimulation, which can be beneficial to one's health. Receptive music therapy is a type of music therapy that includes a period of time spent listening to music mindfully, usually with specially curated recorded or live music [17].

According to studies, music has a positive effect on hormones such as serotonin, dopamine, adrenaline, and testosterone, which are important in the development of mental disorders and regulate our emotional state; it also regulates physiological functions such as blood pressure and breathing [18]. The use of a person's reactions and associations to music in music therapy is used to promote positive improvements in mood and general well-being [19]. Music therapy can include making music with various instruments, singing, dancing to music, or simply listening to it. Music therapy makes use of music's therapeutic properties to help people feel better. It may be used instead of other forms of therapy such as counselling or cognitive behavioural therapy (CBT). Music therapists use a person's reactions and associations to music to promote healthy attitude and mental mindset adjustments. Unconscious emotions are triggered by musical action, and music has a strong connection with them.

The choice of music to employ for stress relief is a personal and unique option. Some people may consider themselves late for work in peak hour traffic, clenching the driving wheel and mumbling curses while tuning the radio to classical music to help them relax. Some could find themselves in the same scenario, but instead choose to shout their favourite pop song loudly. In either case, the decision is yours to make. The first step in de-stressing and reducing stress is to select music, which is one component of the circumstance over which you have influence.

The next stage is to start singing. This is even more personal than music choice, yet it is crucial because it necessitates deep diaphragmatic breathing. Deep breathing, often called abdominal or diaphragmatic breathing which is described in **Figure 1**. As a result, deep breathing and singing can assist to induce relaxation and protect the body from the negative effects of stress.

Music is a soothing therapy that relieves tension and aids in the retrieval of long-forgotten memories [20]. This indicates that music therapy lowered students' tension, implying that students can develop the open-mindedness required in musicological therapy. This is due to the fact that the therapy experiences were creative and reflective abilities were maintained. In the course of therapeutic change, open-mindedness is essential and vital. According to findings, music therapy is useful in lowering anxiety, schizophrenia, physically or mentally challenged individuals, and

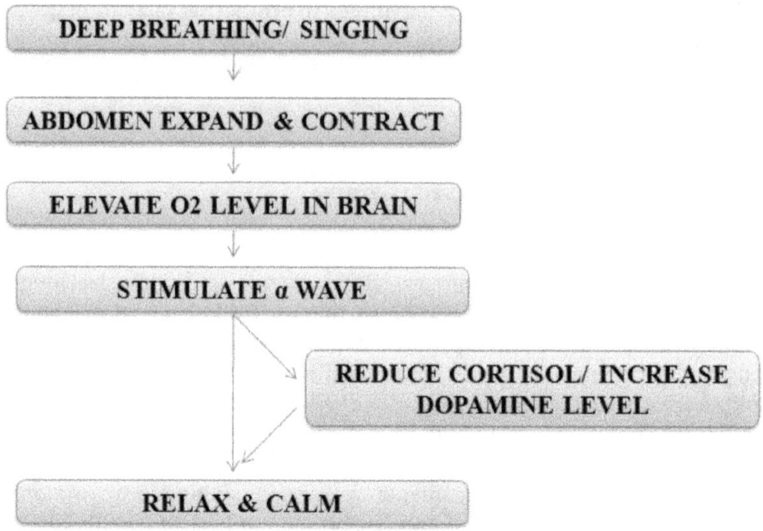

Figure 1.
Mechanism of deep breathing.

school-related stress, among other psychological symptoms [21]. Music therapy's effectiveness addresses emotional issues, naturally increases neurochemicals, rehabilitates individuals with stress and mental illness, improves motor control and well-being, directs physiologic effects through the autonomic nervous system, regulates motor and emotional responses, and positively modifies the release of psychological stress hormones responsible for coordinating the functions of immunity, respiration, and neurology [22]. Music therapy combined with relaxation techniques has been shown in previous research to reduce cognitive stresses of all types, including mild, moderate, and severe stresses [21]. From the previous findings, music can treat all kinds of stress.

4. Music causes neurologic changes in body

Music, which is thought to be a soothing influence at all stages of life, can elicit a wide range of feelings, which can be pleasant or negative depending on the genre of music. Music has been shown in numerous studies to produce major changes in the neurological systems of the brain, as well as changes in brain waves such as beta, theta, alpha, and delta [23]. Music as medicine methods targets specific brain functions and addresses deficiencies that may arise as a result of many of these neurological disorders. Music, rather than being viewed solely as cultural phenomena, should be viewed as a vibration stimulus that causes cognition and memory, according to Siebert et al. [24]. The human brain is programmed to recognise music and respond to rhythm, repetition, tones, and songs. The auditory nerve sends electrical signals from music and other sounds to the temporal lobe's auditory cortex [25]. According to research employing magnetic resonance imaging and positron emission tomography scans, neural networks in various areas of the brain are responsible for decoding and interpreting various aspects of music. Pitch perception, which is the foundation of melody, chords (multiple pitches that sound at the same time), and harmony, requires a small area of the right temporal lobe (two or more melodies at the same time) [26]. Another neighbouring facility

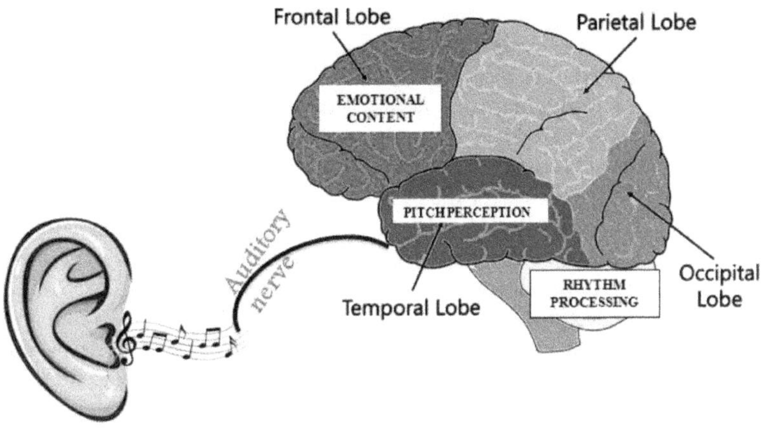

Figure 2.
Recognition of music in brain.

is in charge of deciphering timbre, which is the property that allows the brain to differentiate between different instruments playing the same note [27]. The frontal lobes perceive the emotional content of music, whereas the cerebellum processes rhythm (**Figure 2**). Music that is loud enough to cause "spine tingling" can activate the reward region of the brain, just as enjoyable stimuli such as alcohol or chocolate. Although any healthy human brain is capable of performing all of the complicated processes required to detect music, artists' brains are more finely tuned.

Playing music is more difficult and time-consuming than simply listening to it, although listening to music has been shown to increase cognitive function in the elderly, as well as quality of life and cognition in dementia patients. Depression, anxiety, maniacal states, and thinking and perception abnormalities are the most frequent mental disorders in neurology. Alexithymia, concern, and locus of control are other mental symptoms that can be found in people with neurological diseases [28]. After specific strokes, listening to music can help with cognitive recovery, mood elevation, and muscle function. Singing has been shown to aid in the recovery of speech in aphasic patients. Music-based training can improve gait and balance in senior adults who are at danger of falling; in Parkinson's disease patients, fast, rhythmic music improves gait velocity, cadence, and stride length [28, 29].

One issue in assessing musical illnesses is determining what constitutes a "normal musical brain." While aphasia schedules might legitimately presume a degree of homogeneity in education, where the majority of people are taught to a particular level, the same cannot be said for music. An early study based on differences in melody discrimination depending on whether they were delivered to the left or right ear revealed that musicians and non-musicians have different brain lateralization [30]. A number of neuroimaging studies have revealed structural variations in the auditory [31], motor, somatosensory, superior parietal, callosal, and cerebellar areas of musicians' brains [32]. Longitudinal studies have shown that even brief periods of musical instruction result in functional brain remodelling; however, the extent to which these changes last after training is uncertain [32, 33].

Absolute pitch (AP) musicians have different brain organisation than those [34, 35] who do not have the skill, according to studies. Increases in leftward asymmetry in the PT linked with AP have been shown in structural studies utilising both region-of-interest techniques and whole-brain interrogation with voxel-based morphometry [34]. People without AP show activity in right inferior frontal areas, which might be interpreted as a form of working memory for pitch, whereas AP sufferers engage left dorsolateral frontal areas, which might be seen as associative analysis [34, 35]. The question of whether structural and functional differences in skilled performers are the result of musical training or whether such differences may contribute to an individual's decision to learn music, or to persist in learning music when others may give up, is critical to the interpretation of such differences. The demonstration that the size of the structural difference generally coincides with the age of commencement of musical instruction or the degree of practice supports the thesis that these distinctions originate from, rather than enable, skill development. Only longitudinal studies in which variations in brain structure can be evaluated in the same individuals as learning progresses will be able to unambiguously demonstrate the nature vs. nurture effects [36].

Adolescents were able to relax, increase their identity, improve their emotional problem, reduce their stress, develop and sustain communication, and improve their mental focus, as well as their intellectual and mental growth, using music therapy applications. Listening to music may cause the brain to produce alpha waves, which cause relaxation, or it may boost endorphin release, which causes other physiological responses such as a fall in BP and pulse [37]. Adolescents that abuse substances love rap, hip hop, techno, and dance music [38]. There is additional evidence that rock and metal music, in particular, can have a disastrous impact on young people.

5. Music causes endocrinological changes in body

Music was generally agreed to lower cortisol levels, whether through direct engagement or listening to recorded music. Only a couple research found the reverse trend, but in both cases, the music group's growth was less than the control group [39]. Both relaxing and stimulating music reduced cortisol levels, whereas few studies stated that only a drop for relaxing music and an increase for stimulating music. This was reflected in the study's measurements of GH and ACTH, as well as a comparable response from epinephrine, which increased when exposed to stimulating music but remained unaltered when exposed to calming music. These findings suggest that hormones are sensitive to musical stimulus [40]. When participants listened to soothing recorded music, oxytocin levels increased more than the other hormones examined. Bittman et al. revealed an increase in the dehydroepiandrosterone (DHEA) to cortisol ratio when participants participated in group drumming, whereas Conrad et al. observed a decrease in the DHEA to cortisol ratio and a rise in growth hormone when patients listened to relaxing recorded music [41, 42]. Migneault et al. reported that when participants chose their own recorded music, testosterone levels elevated in men but dropped in women [43].

6. Link between stress, memory, and music therapy

Memory is one of the CNS's most significant functions, and it is divided into sensory, short-term, and long-term memory. Stress has been proven to create functional and structural alterations in the hippocampal area of the brain. Chronic stress, which results in a rise in plasma cortisol level, reduces the number of dendritic branches and neurons in the hippocampus, as well as structural abnormalities in synaptic terminals and impaired neurogenesis [44, 45]. Declarative memory impairments can be caused by high levels of stress hormones [46]. Stress has a negative impact on learning as well. After a stressful event, the memory-building process is frequently reinforced [47].

Physiologically, music can also increase the heart rate and hormone levels of patients with cognitive impairment [48]. In addition, playing musical instruments can delay the onset of cognitive decline in the future and reduce the risk of dementia. Therefore, music seems to be a necessity for patients with dementia [49]. Singing is also commonly used to help people with dementia. They discovered that sad music was the most efficient for recalling personal experiences, particularly distant ones. This revealed that the emotional content of music played a significant influence in the dementia recall memory process [50]. In addition to medicine for dementia, there is a growing trend in research using a multimodal stimulation intervention, which combines several different cognitive stimulations. Ozdemir and his colleagues created multimodal stimulations for mild AD patients, including MT with a light tempo instrument, painting lifeless alive drawings, and orientation to time-place-person. This study found that multi-domain stimulation enhanced MMSE scores while lowering Geriatric Depression Scale and Beck Anxiety Scale scores [51].

A vast amount of research indicates that music therapy improves behaviour, anxiety, mood, and memory in dementia patients. Short-term music therapy has been demonstrated to be useful in reducing mood symptoms such as depression and anxiety, while longer-term music therapy has also been proved to be quite effective. Another research revealed that personalised music therapy has therapeutic benefits on anxiety and depression.

7. Stress and music therapy for Alzheimer disease

Progressive cognitive impairment reduces the stress threshold. As a result, under stressful circumstances, patients may exhibit agitation or aggressive behaviour [52]. Music therapy helps people become more tolerant of stressful environmental cues that can cause these symptoms [53]. Music-related feelings appear to be preserved in people with Alzheimer disease (AD). Brain regions involved in music recognition are mostly unaffected by Alzheimer's disease, and music may help persons with the disease remember their own lives better. According to the literature, music improves the encoding of verbal information in both healthy older people and Alzheimer's sufferers [54]. Music therapy, a combination of "therapist" and "listening to music", has the greatest effect on patients with Alzheimer's disease in the early stages, as contrasted to the ones used alone. The increases in 17-estradiol and testosterone levels seen in Alzheimer's patients with declining hormones show that music therapy may help to slow or even stop the progression of Alzheimer's disease. Music therapy is thought to restore normal hormone levels, reduce nerve cell damage, and protect nerve cells, halting progression. For healthy elderly people, music therapy could be an effective Alzheimer's disease prevention strategy [55].

Perceptual-motor issues are common in people with Alzheimer's disease, and they may become restless at particular times of the day. Exercise can help them feel less restless. People feel better when they are physically active. Exercising to music promotes the use of various body parts, improves circulation, promotes attention, and aids in the release of tension and extra energy. Perhaps most importantly, music is a pleasurable, uplifting, and sociable experience [56]. When compared to the waitlist control group, individuals who received music therapy with a relaxation programme had considerably lower stress levels. Music therapy and relaxation programmes were also proven to have a favourable effect.

8. Conclusion

When paired with standard of care, music therapy is a viable and effective treatment for a wide range of diseases. It works as an anxiolytic and can also help with stress relief. Music is a strong medium that we may use in our daily lives to improve our quality of life as we age. Maintaining wellness through active music creation is a terrific compliment to proper nutrition and exercise, regular doctor appointments, having a positive mindset, and engagement in religion or spirituality.

Author details

Gayatri Devi Ramalingam[1*], G. Sridevi[1], Jothi Priya Amirtham[1], Preetha Santhakumar[1] and S. Saravanakumar[2]

1 Department of Physiology, Saveetha Dental College and Hospitals, SIMATS, Chennai, India

2 Department of Anatomy, SEGI University, Petaling Jaya, Malaysia

*Address all correspondence to: gayatri.physio88@gmail.com

References

[1] Selye H. The stress of life. Revised Edition 1984. New York: McGraw-Hill; 1956

[2] Trumper M. Bodily Changes in Pain, Hunger, Fear and Rage: An Account of Recent Researches into the Function of Emotional Excitement. Psychology Clinical. 1930;**19**(3):100-101

[3] Lacey JI, Lacey BC. Verification and extension of the principle of autonomic response-stereotypy. The American Journal of Psychology. 1958;**71**(1):50-73

[4] Shaw JA. Children exposed to war/terrorism. Clinical Child and Family Psychology Review. 2003;**6**(4):237-246

[5] McNally RJ. Psychological mechanisms in acute response to trauma. Biological Psychiatry. 2003;**53**(9):779-788. DOI: 10.1016/s0006-3223(02)01663-3

[6] Vahia VN. Diagnostic and statistical manual of mental disorders 5: A quick glance. Indian Journal of Psychiatry. 2013;**55**(3):220-223

[7] Colby JP Jr, Linsky AS, Straus MA. Social stress and state-to-state differences in smoking and smoking related mortality in the United States. Social Science & Medicine. 1994;**38**(2): 373-381

[8] Selye H. Stress in Health and Disease. Boston: Butterworth-Heinemann; 2013

[9] Bernardi L. Cardiovascular, cerebrovascular, and respiratory changes induced by different types of music in musicians and non-musicians: the importance of silence. Heart. 2005;**92**(4):445-452. DOI: 10.1136/hrt.2005.064600

[10] Good M, Picot BL, Salem SG, Chin C-C, Picot SF, Lane D. Cultural differences in music chosen for pain relief. Journal of Holistic Nursing. 2000;**18**(3):245-260. DOI: 10.1177/089801010001800306

[11] Arnon S, Shapsa A, Forman L, Regev R, Bauer S, Litmanovitz I, et al. Live music is beneficial to preterm infants in the neonatal intensive care unit environment. Birth. 2006;**33**(2): 131-136

[12] Baker F, Uhlig S, editors. Voicework in Music Therapy: Research and Practice. London: Jessica Kingsley Publishers; 2011

[13] Chanda ML, Levitin DJ. The neurochemistry of music. Trends in Cognitive Sciences. 2013;17(4):179-193. DOI: 10.1016/j.tics.2013.02.007

[14] Nilsson U. The anxiety- and pain-reducing effects of music interventions: A systematic review. AORN Journal. 2008;**87**(4):780-807. DOI: 10.1016/j.aorn.2007.09.013

[15] Thaut MH, Hoemberg V, editors. Handbook of Neurologic Music Therapy. Oxford: OUP; 2014

[16] Hanser SB. Music therapy and stress reduction research. Journal of Music Therapy. 1985;**22**(4):193-206. DOI: 10.1093/jmt/22.4.193

[17] Stegemann T, Geretsegger M, Phan Quoc E, Riedl H, Smetana M. Music Therapy and Other Music-Based Interventions in Pediatric Health Care: An Overview. Medicines (Basel). 2019;**6**(1):25

[18] Dowson B, McDermott O. Approaches to measuring the impact of music therapy and music activities on people living with dementia. In: Baird A, Garrido S, Tamplin J, editors. Music and Dementia: From Cognition to Therapy. 1st ed. New York: Oxford

University Press; 2019. pp. 171-196. DOI: 10.1093/oso/9780190075934.003.0009

[19] Lindsay M. Music therapy in dementia care Aldridge David (Ed) Music therapy in dementia care 256pp Jessica Kingsley 9781853027765 1853027766. Nursing Standard. 2001;**15**:29. DOI: 10.7748/ns2001.06.15.41.29.b1

[20] Mohammad NR. Effect of music therapy on stress: Is it really effective? International Journal of Emergency Mental Health and Human Resilience. 2015;17(2):446. DOI: 10.4172/1522-4821.1000192

[21] Raglio A. Effects of music and music therapy on mood in neurological patients. World Journal of Psychiatry. 2015;**5**(1):68. DOI: 10.5498/wjp.v5.i1.68

[22] Ezegbe BN, Ede MO, Eseadi C, Nwaubani OO, Akaneme IN, Aye EN, et al. Effect of music therapy combined with cognitive restructuring therapy on emotional distress in a sample of Nigerian married couples. Medicine. 2018;**97**(34):e11637. DOI: 10.1097/md.0000000000011637

[23] Musacchia G, Khalil A. Music and Learning: Does Music Make You Smarter?. Frontiers for Young Minds. 2020;**8**:81

[24] Siebert M, Markowitsch HJ, Bartel P. Amygdala, affect and cognition: Evidence from 10 patients with Urbach-Wiethe disease. Brain: A Journal of Neurology. 2003;**126**(Pt. 12):2627-2637

[25] Radstaak M, Geurts SA, Brosschot JF, Kompier MA. Music and psychophysiological recovery from stress. Psychosomatic Medicine. 2014;**76**(7):529-537. DOI: 10.1097/psy.0000000000000094

[26] Stewart L, von Kriegstein K, Warren JD, Griffiths TD. Music and the brain: Disorders of musical listening. Brain. 2006;**129**(10):2533-2553. DOI: 10.1093/brain/awl171

[27] Münte TF, Kohlmetz C, Nager W, Altenmüller E. Neuroperception. Superior auditory spatial tuning in conductors. Nature. 2001;**409**(6820):580

[28] Hemming L et al. Alexithymia and its associations with depression, suicidality, and aggression: An overview of the literature. Frontiers in Psychiatry. 2019;**10**:203

[29] de Bruin N et al. Walking with music is a safe and viable tool for gait training in Parkinson's disease: The effect of a 13-week feasibility study on single and dual task walking. Parkinson's Disease. 2010;**2010**:483530

[30] Spiegel MF, Watson CS. Performance on frequency-discrimination tasks by musicians and nonmusicians. The Journal of the Acoustical Society of America. 1984;**76**(6):1690-1695. DOI: 10.1121/1.391605

[31] Schneider P et al. Morphology of Heschl's gyrus reflects enhanced activation in the auditory cortex of musicians. Nature Neuroscience. 2002;**5**(7):688-694. DOI: 10.1038/nn871

[32] Gaab N et al. Functional anatomy of pitch memory—An fMRI study with sparse temporal sampling. NeuroImage. 2003;**19**(4):1417-1426. DOI: 10.1016/s1053-8119(03)00224-6

[33] Hutchinson S. Cerebellar volume of musicians. Cerebral Cortex. 2003;**13**:943-949. DOI: 10.1093/cercor/13.9.943

[34] Luders E et al. A voxel-based approach to gray matter asymmetries. NeuroImage. 2004;**22**(2):656-664. DOI: 10.1016/j.neuroimage.2004.01.032

[35] Zatorre RJ et al. Functional anatomy of musical processing in listeners with

absolute pitch and relative pitch. Proceedings of the National Academy of Sciences. 1998;**95**(6):3172-3177. DOI: 10.1073/pnas.95.6.3172

[36] Amunts K et al. Motor cortex and hand motor skills: Structural compliance in the human brain. Human Brain Mapping. 1997;**5**(3):206-215. DOI: 10.1002/(sici)1097-0193(1997)5: 3<206::aid-hbm5>3.0.co;2-7

[37] Yildirim D, Özbek A. Erken Dönem Ekonomi Eğitimi ve Finansal Sosyalizasyonun Finansal Okuryazarlık Düzeyine Etkisi. Afyon Kocatepe Üniversitesi Sosyal Bilimler Dergisi. 2021;**23**(2):694-710. DOI: 10.32709/akusosbil.860749

[38] Önal A, Ögel K, Eke C. Dikkat Eksikliği ve Hiperaktivite Belirtileri Bulunan Ergenlerde Madde Kullanımı ve Aile Özellikleri Üstüne Kesitsel Bir Çalışma. Klinik Psikofarmakoloji Bulteni-Bulletin of Clinical Psychopharmacology. 2011;**21**(3):225-231. DOI: 10.5455/bcp.20110627104419

[39] Escher J et al. Music during gastroscopy. Schweizerische Medizinische Wochenschrift. 1993;**123**(26):1354-1358

[40] Fancourt D, Ockelford A, Belai A. The psychoneuroimmunological effects of music: A systematic review and a new model. Brain, Behavior, and Immunity. 2014;**36**:15-26. DOI: 10.1016/j.bbi.2013.10.014

[41] Bittman BB et al. Composite effects of group drumming music therapy on modulation of neuroendocrine-immune parameters in normal subjects. Alternative Therapies in Health and Medicine. 2001;**7**(1):38-47

[42] Conrad C et al. Overture for growth hormone: Requiem for interleukin-6?*. Critical Care Medicine. 2007;**35**(12): 2709-2713. DOI: 10.1097/00003246-200712000-00005

[43] Migneault B et al. The effect of music on the neurohormonal stress response to surgery under general anesthesia. Anesthesia & Analgesia. 2004;**98**(2):527-532. DOI: 10.1213/01.ane.0000096182.70239.23

[44] Sapolsky RM et al. Hippocampal damage associated with prolonged glucocorticoid exposure in primates. The Journal of Neuroscience: The Official Journal of the Society for Neuroscience. 1990;**10**(9):2897-2902

[45] Woolley CS, Gould E, McEwen BS. Exposure to excess glucocorticoids alters dendritic morphology of adult hippocampal pyramidal neurons. Brain Research. 1990;**531**(1-2):225-231

[46] Steckler T, Kalin NH, JMH R, editors. Handbook of Stress and the Brain Part 1: The Neurobiology of Stress. Amsterdam: Elsevier; 2005

[47] Schwabe L et al. Stress effects on memory: An update and integration. Neuroscience & Biobehavioral Reviews. 2012;**36**(7):1740-1749. DOI: 10.1016/j.neubiorev.2011.07.002

[48] Baird A, Garrido S, Tamplin J, editors. Music and Dementia: From Cognition to Therapy. London: Oxford University Press; 2019

[49] Verghese J et al. Leisure activities and the risk of dementia in the elderly. New England Journal of Medicine. 2003;**348**(25):2508-2516. DOI: 10.1056/nejmoa022252

[50] Vanstone AD, Cuddy LL. Melody, memory, and engagement in Alzheimer's disease. In: Baird A, Garrido S, Tamplin J, editors. Music and Dementia: From Cognition to Therapy. New York: Oxford University Press; 2019. pp. 67-87. DOI: 10.1093/oso/9780190075934.003.0004

[51] Ozdemir L, Akdemir N. Effects of multisensory stimulation on cognition, depression and anxiety levels of

mildly-affected Alzheimer's patients. Journal of the Neurological Sciences. 2009;**283**(1-2):211-213. DOI: 10.1016/j.jns.2009.02.367

[52] Smith M et al. History, development, and future of the progressively lowered stress threshold: A conceptual model for dementia care. Journal of the American Geriatrics Society. 2004;**52**(10):1755-1760. DOI: 10.1111/j.1532-5415.2004.52473.x

[53] Volicer L, Hurley AC. Management of behavioral symptoms in progressive degenerative dementias. The Journals of Gerontology Series A: Biological Sciences and Medical Sciences. 2003;**58**(9):M837-M845. DOI: 10.1093/gerona/58.9.m837

[54] Simmons-Stern NR, Budson AE, Ally BA. Music as a memory enhancer in patients with Alzheimer's disease. Neuropsychologia. 2010;**48**(10): 3164-3167. DOI: 10.1016/j.neuropsychologia.2010.04.033

[55] Fukui H, Arai A, Toyoshima K. Efficacy of music therapy in treatment for the patients with Alzheimer's disease. International Journal of Alzheimer's Disease. 2012;**2012**:531646. DOI: 10.1155/2012/531646

[56] Petersson G, Nyström M. Music therapy as a caring intervention: Swedish musicians learning a new professional field. International Journal of Music Education. 2011;**29**(1):3-14. DOI: 10.1177/0255761410389659

Section 4

Perception Related to Prostate Cancer

Chapter 5

Health-seeking Behaviours and Effect of Prostate Cancer on Male Soldiers in Ghana: A Qualitative Study

Emmanuel Anongeba Anaba, Juliana Gyasi Necku and Moses Abile

Abstract

Prostate cancer is a global public health problem and contributes to the global morbidity and mortality burden. This study aimed to explore health-seeking behaviours and the effect of prostate cancer on Ghanaian soldiers. This study employed a phenomenology qualitative research design. In-depth interviews were conducted among 24 male soldiers living with prostate cancer. Data were collected with the aid of an interview guide and analysed using qualitative thematic analysis. Three major themes and ten subthemes emerged from the thematic analysis. The three major themes were diagnosis, treatment and effects of prostate cancer. The subthemes under diagnosis were medical tests and symptoms of prostate cancer. The subthemes under treatment were orthodox treatment, herbal treatment and behaviour change. The subthemes under effect were poor physical, sexual, mental, social and financial wellbeing. Ghanaian soldiers living with prostate cancer adopt multiple health-seeking behaviours. Prostate cancer adversely affects the physical, sexual, mental and social wellbeing as well as the financial stability of soldiers. This study provides relevant information for public health policy and programming.

Keywords: Ghana, prostate cancer, soldier, qualitative study, health-seeking, effects

1. Introduction

Prostate cancer (PC) is a global public health problem. PC is the second most common cause of cancer deaths among Whites, African Americans, American Indians and Hispanic men [1]. Estimates suggest that by 2030, 1.7 million new cases of PC and 499,000 related deaths will occur if the trend is not interrupted [2]. Several studies have shown that occupational exposures are risk factors of prostate cancer [3], besides race, family history and age. Soldiers are more likely to be diagnosed with prostate cancer compared with the general population [4]. Partly because, they are more exposed to cancer-causing agents, such as pesticides, metals, chemicals, radiation, warfare chemical, fuels and solvent, compared with the general population [5]. Moreover, soldiers are more exposed to cadmium, which is a risk factor for prostate cancer. Cadmium is used in military installations, including surface treatment in aerospace and weapons systems to prevent corrosion.

Further, soldiers are frequently exposed to sunlight and physical fitness coupled with unhealthy behaviours, such as smoking, alcohol consumption and unhealthy diets, which predispose them to prostate cancer [4]. Also, military deployment is associated with immunization and depletion of uranium which increases soldiers' risk of prostate cancer [6]. Besides, soldiers are more likely to have access to free health care, frequent contact with doctors, hence are more likely to get screened for prostate cancer. The frequent medical examination is common among the military, which contributes to the detection of more prostate cancer cases among soldiers. However, evidence shows that soldiers have negative attitudes towards seeking health care services [7].

Soldiers provide essential services (i.e., protect life and property), hence promoting their health and wellbeing is crucial. Prostate cancer has the potential to negatively affect the health, wellbeing and productivity of soldiers. Studies have shown that prostate cancer is associated with physical and cognitive disabilities, which negatively affect job performance [8, 9]. Prostate cancer is also associated with sexual dysfunction [10]. Therefore, the impact of prostate cancer on soldiers cannot be underestimated.

In Ghana, prostate cancer is the second leading cause of cancer deaths. One in three Ghanaian men of age 40 and above are at risk of prostate cancer [11]. The rising prevalence of prostate cancer in the country is a public health threat. However, there is a paucity of empirical evidence on the subject matter. For instance, Ghana has no published cancer register and no well-established policy guidelines for prostate cancer management, making it difficult to accurately estimate the burden of the disease.

A majority of the military personnel in Ghana are males, hence are at risk of prostate cancer. The 37 Military Hospital (the largest military hospital in Ghana) records new cases of prostate cancer among soldiers every year. Yet, there is rare evidence of Ghanaian soldiers living with prostate cancer. Also, existing studies on prostate cancer are largely quantitative studies, hence little is known about the experiences of prostate cancer survivors. Generating empirical evidence on the phenomenon is crucial for public health policy and programming. The objective of this study was to explore health-seeking behaviours and the effect of prostate cancer among male soldiers in Ghana.

2. Methods

This study was conducted in the 37 Military Hospital, the largest military healthcare facility in Ghana. It is also the 37th military hospital to be built in the British colony of West Africa. The hospital is located in Accra, Ghana's capital city. The hospital has a total bed capacity of 400 and serves as one of the referral hospitals in the coastal part of Ghana.

The Ghana Armed Forces comprise the Navy, Army and Air Force. More than half of the military personnel are males. This study focused on male soldiers who have been diagnosed with prostate cancer and were receiving treatment in the 37 Military Hospital. With the assistance of health professionals in the hospital, respondents were selected using the purposive sampling technique during hospital visits. We adopted a phenomenology qualitative research design.

Respondents who consented were interviewed in a private room by the first author with the aid of an interview guide. All the interviews were conducted in the English Language because all the respondents were literate. The average duration for the interviews was about forty (40) minutes. The first author visited the hospital bi-weekly, except at weekends to interview respondents. A discussion approach was employed to conduct the interviews coupled with several inductive probes

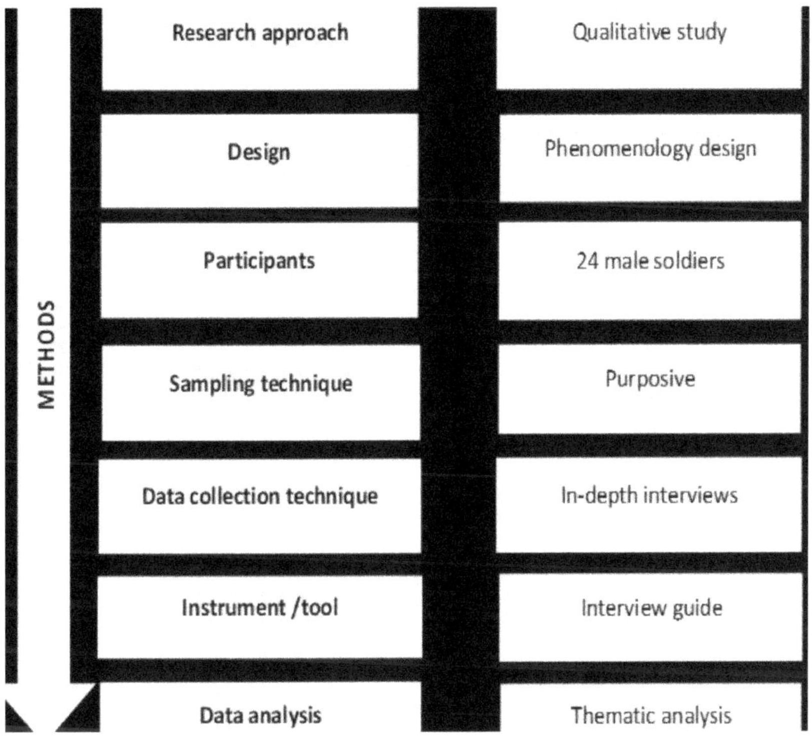

Figure 1.
Schematic diagram of methods.

to broaden the narratives as much as possible. With the consent of participants, interviews were audiotaped coupled with taking notes. Data saturation was attained after interviewing 24 respondents. Before data collection, approval was sought from the management of the hospital. Also, the purpose of the study was made known to the respondents as well as their right to voluntarily participate or redraw from the study at any stage. We obtained written consent from all the respondents as well as assured them of privacy and confidentiality.

Thematic analysis was employed to identify themes within the data. The analysis was guided by Braun and Clarke's thematic analysis framework [12]. Audio recordings were listened to severally and transcribed by the first author, while the second author verified the transcripts by comparing it with the recordings. To gain familiarization with the data as well as document initial impression, both the transcripts and the notes were read severally by all the authors. Afterwards, parts of the transcripts were coded manually to identify the main themes. Coding was done separately by the authors and subsequently compared, discussed and revised where necessary. Codes that fitted were grouped into themes after serious scrutiny and revised to safeguard consistency between themes and related data. Lastly, the themes were well-defined into main and sub-themes. Findings were presented according to main and sub-themes and verbatim quotes were selected at random (**Figure 1**).

3. Results

Out of the 24 respondents, 54% were between the ages of 51 and 60 years, 92% were married and 58% had attained tertiary education. Moreover, 54% of the

Characteristic n = 24	n (%)
Age (years)	
41–50	11 (46)
51–60	13 (54)
Marital status	
Married	22 (92)
Divorced	29 (8)
Education	
Secondary school	10 (42)
Tertiary	14 (58)
Rank	
Officer	13 (54)
Non-officer	11 (46)
Religion	
Christianity	12 (50)
Islam	8 (33)
No religion	4 (17)
Work experience (years)	
1–10	3 (13)
11–20	7 (29)
21–30	9 (37)
31–35	5 (21)

Table 1.
Characteristics of participants.

respondents were officers, 50% professed Christianity and 37% had between 21 and 30 years of work experience (**Table 1**).

From the thematic analysis, three main themes emerged, including diagnosis, treatment and effects of prostate cancer. Two subthemes emerged under-diagnosis, including medical tests and symptoms of prostate cancer. Three subthemes emerged under treatment, including orthodox treatment, herbal treatment and behaviour change. Five subthemes emerged under the effects of prostate cancer, including poor physical, sexual, mental, social and financial wellbeing (**Table 2**).

3.1 Diagnosis

3.1.1 Medical test for diagnosing prostate cancer

All the respondents stated that they were diagnosed by health professionals using various medical tests/examinations. Probing further, some respondents revealed that they underwent Prostate-Specific Antigen (PSA), Digital Rectal Examination (DRE) and Biopsy tests to confirm the presence of cancer in the prostate gland. The soldiers indicated that the medical tests were prescribed by health practitioners when they visited the hospital with signs and symptoms of prostate cancer. This is what a respondent had to say about how he got to know his PC status.

Main theme	Subtheme
Diagnosis of prostate cancer	Medical tests—Prostate Specific Antigen Test (PSA), Digital Rectal Examination (DRE) and Biopsy test
	Symptoms of prostate cancer—painful micturition, frequent micturition, blood in urine, weak urinary stream, pain during ejaculation, difficulty in postponing urine, abdominal pains.
Treatment of prostate cancer	Orthodox treatment—hormonal therapy, Radical prostatectomy,
	Herbal/traditional—herbal medication
	Behaviour change—changes in diet and alcohol consumption
Effects of prostate cancer	Physical wellbeing—weight loss
	Sexual wellbeing—poor sexual performance
	Mental wellbeing—depression, insomnia
	Social wellbeing—dependency, isolation
	Economic wellbeing—catastrophic healthcare expenditure, poor job performance

Table 2.
Main themes and subthemes from thematic analysis.

> *"I reported to my doctor about pains in my scrotum. He then requested for PSA test, DRE and biopsy test. Through the following tests, it was confirmed by the doctor that I have prostate cancer" (Participant 5, Non-officer).*

3.1.2 Symptoms of prostate cancer

The respondents stated that they experienced painful urination, frequent urination, especially at night, urinary retention, blood in urine, weak urinary stream, painful ejaculation, difficulty in postponing urine, abdominal pains and burning sensations after urination. This was what a respondent had to say:

> *"I had a weak urinary stream, a lot of pain during urination and sometimes I saw blood in my urine" (Participant 15, Non-officer).*

3.2 Treatment for prostate cancer

3.2.1 Orthodox treatment

Most of the respondents specified that they were undergoing hormonal therapy, while other respondents indicated that they were undergoing Radical prostatectomy. According to one respondent:

> *"After I was diagnosed with prostate cancer some years ago, I have been on hormonal therapy all this while" (Participant 21, Officer).*

3.2.2 Traditional/ herbal treatment

The soldiers combined both orthodox and herbal medicines to treat prostate cancer. This suggests that there is the practice of medical pluralism in managing prostate cancer. This was what a soldier said:

> *"I was diagnosed with prostate cancer about a year ago and I have been on hormonal therapy and herbal treatment. I think the two would be more effective than just depending on only one method" (Participant 8, Non-officer).*

3.2.3 Behaviour change

Besides, orthodox and herbal treatments, the respondents expressed divergent views regarding changes in behaviour. Some respondents underscored that they have adopted positive health behaviours, such as quitting smoking, reducing the intake of alcohol and unhealthy diets. One respondent said:

> *"For me to recover fast, I decided to stop bad eating habits, alcohol intake and smoking. I have reduced my dietary intake to help me recover well" (Participant 13, Non-officer).*

3.3 Effects of prostate cancer

3.3.1 Poor physical wellbeing

The soldiers indicated that the disease has affected their physical health. Some respondents expressed concerns about weight loss due to prostate cancer. A respondent lamented that:

> *"I have lost some weight due to my condition couple with urinal incontinence" (Participant 3, Officer).*

3.3.2 Poor sexual wellbeing

The soldiers lamented about poor sexual functioning. The respondents stated that they could not get an erection or keep an erection during sexual intercourse, experienced pain and discomfort during and after ejaculation, as well as did not enjoy sex anymore. For example, a respondent stated that:

> *"My condition has affected my sexual performance very badly. I find it difficult to erect and after managing to erect, I don't stay long at all. Moreover, there is this pain and discomfort I usually experience during ejaculation and it is disturbing me so much" (Participant 1, Officer).*

3.3.3 Poor social wellbeing

The respondents also lamented that the disease has affected their social wellbeing. A reduction in respondents' engagement in social events, such as festivals, weddings, funerals, was common. Respondents who participated in social gatherings before the onset of prostate cancer stated that they could no longer participate in social events. Some respondents bemoaned that they could not attend social gatherings due to frequent urination and urine incontinence, while other respondents expressed concerns about how they could no longer socialize with friends. According to one respondent;

> *"Because I cannot postpone urination, I do not want to socialize anymore. This is because, I might end up embarrassing myself in public, at first, I use to engage in sporting activities but of late I cannot do that anymore due to the disease am having" (Participant 19, Officer).*

3.3.4 Poor mental wellbeing

Prostate cancer was associated with poor mental wellbeing. The respondents indicated that they experienced stress, insomnia, anxiety and severe depression. A soldier expressed the following concern.

> *"I usually have insomnia; thus, I cannot sleep well in the night and have to wake up several times before is morning" (Participant 22, Officer).*

3.3.5 Poor financial wellbeing

The respondents stated that they pay their medical bills, which poses a huge financial burden on them and their families. Some respondents depend on relatives and friends for money to pay their medical bills. A respondent stated that:

> *"I spend a lot on medical bills and cannot even afford the prescribed treatment. For instance, I cannot afford the hormonal treatment due to financial constraints" (Participant 6, Non-officer).*

Also, respondents indicated that the cost of treatment for prostate cancer was very expensive, making it very difficult for them to access. Soldiers who had enrolled in the National Health Insurance Scheme (NHIS) said they still pay out-of-pocket for medication because treatment for prostate cancer is not included in the benefits package. Hence, the respondents who had enrolled in the NHIS did not have any protection against catastrophic healthcare expenditure. A respondent said:

> *"The cost of treatment is very expensive. I cannot afford and sometimes have to depend on friends and families to support me. In fact, it has not been easy for me". (Participant 20, Non-officer).*

The soldiers stated that prostate cancer affected their performance on the job. For example, some soldiers could not engage in regular physical activity, while other respondents absent from work.

> *"My condition has affected my performance negatively. I cannot work like before; I easily get tired and sometimes lose my concentration on the job due to worrying about my condition" (Participant 4, Non-officer).*

4. Discussion

Three main themes emerged from the thematic analysis, including diagnosis, treatment and effects of prostate cancer. Regarding diagnosis, three main medical tests were employed by health professionals to diagnose soldiers who visited the hospital with symptoms such as painful micturition, frequent micturition, blood in urine, weak urinary stream and painful ejaculation. These medical tests include the Prostate-Specific Antigen test, Digital Rectal Examination and Biopsy test. These findings corroborate with findings of prior studies [10, 13]. The above tests are widely known for diagnosing prostate cancer [13]. This is commendable, however not surprising, because the 37 Military Hospital is a referral hospital. Therefore, it is expected that the hospital should have ultra-modern medical technology coupled with cancer specialists. This implies that soldiers in Ghana have access to standard prostate cancer diagnosis which conforms to international best practices.

In addition, multiple therapies were adopted to cure prostate cancer, including orthodox and herbal medicines coupled with changes in behaviour. Hormonal treatment and Radical prostatectomy were the common medical treatment options for soldiers with prostate cancer. Besides, soldiers preferred both orthodox and herbal treatments (medical pluralism), which is a common practice among the general

Ghanaian population [14]. This finding requires urgent attention since medical pluralism can negatively affect treatment outcomes. It was insightful to find that soldiers had adopted positive health behaviours to aid in their recovery, including healthy dietary practices, physical activity and cessation of smoking. In this regard, we recommend that a multi-disciplinary approach to prostate cancer treatment, such as incorporating dietitians, physical activity specialists and counsellors in the continuum of care, should be adopted.

Furthermore, prostate cancer affected soldiers' physical, sexual, mental, social and financial wellbeing. These findings are parallel with existing studies [15, 16]. Evidence shows that depression is common among persons living with prostate cancer [17]. Again, there is evidence to show that prostate cancer is associated with weight loss [18]. Persons living with prostate cancer experience erectile dysfunction [13], which affects their masculinity and emotional wellbeing. For instance, a similar study found that men living with prostate cancer experienced difficulties with ejaculation, erection, urination and orgasm [19]. Also, prostate cancer had financial implications, including poor job performance and the high cost of treatment [20]. The cost of treatment for prostate cancer was perceived to be expensive, predisposing soldiers to catastrophic healthcare expenditure. Research shows that prostate cancer is associated with financial hardships [21]. These findings imply that soldiers living with prostate cancer need medical, emotional, social and financial support. It is therefore crucial for stakeholders to design strategies and programmes to help minimize the adverse effects of prostate cancer on soldiers.

We recommend that stakeholders should adopt a multi-disciplinary approach to help minimize the adverse effects of prostate cancer. For instance, the cost of treatment for prostate cancer should be included in the benefits package of Ghana's National Health Insurance Scheme. Although, the cost of treatment for cervical and breast cancer is covered by the National Health Insurance Scheme, the cost of treatment for prostate cancer is currently not covered. This can help provide financial risk protection to persons living with prostate cancer. Alternatively, the management of the Ghana Armed Forces should consider providing financial support to soldiers living with prostate cancer, such as paying their medical bills. In addition, healthcare providers should educate prostate cancer patients about risks associated with medical pluralism as well as provide counselling services for soldiers with emotional problems. Also, it is crucial to involve psychologists and sex therapists in the continuum of care to provide support services to prostate cancer patients experiencing sexual dysfunction. There is therefore a need for multi-stakeholder collaboration, such as the Ghana Armed Forces, the Ghana Health Services, the National Health Insurance Authority and the Ghana Psychological Association.

Although, the findings of this study provide valuable information for health policies and programming, it is not devoid of limitations. Firstly, the findings of the study must be interpreted with caution, since the study was conducted among few soldiers. Also, the findings of the study cannot be generalized due to the qualitative nature and small sample size. Therefore, future studies should adopt longitudinal designs and a large sample size. Notwithstanding, this is the maiden study to explore the lived experiences of Ghanaian soldiers living with prostate cancer.

5. Conclusion

This study demonstrated that Ghanaian soldiers living with prostate cancer adopt multiple health-seeking behaviours. Prostate cancer adversely affects the physical, sexual, mental and social wellbeing as well as the financial stability of soldiers. These findings are consistent with the findings of previous studies. The findings of this study provide relevant information for public health policy and programming. Going forward, a multidisciplinary approach should be adopted to help promote the health and wellbeing of soldiers living with prostate cancer.

Acknowledgements

The author would like to thank the management of the Ghana Armed Forces for permitting them to collect data from their organization. Also, we thank all the respondents who sacrificed their time and energy to participate in the interviews.

Conflict of interest

The authors declare no conflict of interest.

Appendix

Consent form

Section A: Background information

Title of Study	Assessing the impact of prostate cancer on the health security of soldiers. A case study of the Ghana Armed Forces.
Principal Investigator:	Juliana Gyasi Necku

Section B: Consent to participate in research

General Information about research

Prostate cancer is the most common non-skin cancer among men and the sixth leading cause of cancer-related death among men globally. Estimations indicate that by 2030, 1.7 million new cases of prostate cancer will be recorded coupled with 499,000 new deaths. Prostate cancer can pose a serious threat to health security, which is an essential part of human security. Prostate cancer is the second leading cause of cancer deaths among men in Ghana. Out of every three men of 40 years and above in Ghana, one is at risk of prostate cancer. This is a cross-sectional survey that seeks to assess men understanding, attitudes, health-seeking behaviours and impact of prostate cancer. This study will last for three months and it is expected that you will be available during the study period for interviews.

Benefits/Risks of the study

Benefits: There is no direct benefit for you. However, findings from this study will help promote the reproductive health and wellbeing of men through policies and programmes. It will also help improve stakeholders' understanding of prostate cancer and access to professional healthcare services for men living with prostate cancer.

Risks: You will be required to answer questions about yourself and your experiences about prostate cancer, hence there will be minimal risk and discomfort. You can contact the Principal Investigator (Juliana Gyasi Necku) on +233 244284669 to channel your concerns. Also, there is a counselor on standby to counsel you with support if you experience any emotional challenges.

Confidentiality

We will protect information about you to the best of our ability. Information provided by you will be saved on a computer with a password so no one else can see it. Your real name and other identifiable information will not be shared with anyone else and you will be given a study identity number with which we will identify you. The interview will be audio recorded for it to be transcribed into word format. This recording will not have any record of your name or any easily identifiable information. It will only be available to the research team. The findings will be reported in a thesis report and submitted to the Ghana Armed Forces Command and Staff College as well as disseminated in scientific journals and conferences. This study is strictly for academic purposes and your name or any identifiable information will not appear in any publication or presentation.

Compensation

There will be no monetary compensation for you if you agree to participate in this study.

Withdrawal from study

Your participation in this study is voluntary and you can drop out at any time of the study period if you wish to end your participation. You or your legal representative will be informed promptly if information becomes available that may be relevant to your willingness to continue participation or withdraw. You may do so without any consequences.

Contact for additional information

Please for further information about this project or related injuries, contact the:

Student Investigator

Juliana Gyasi Necku
Ghana Armed Forces Staff Command College, Accra
Tel: +233 244284669
Email: adjoanecku@gmail.com

Section C: Participant agreement

"I have read or have had someone read all of the above, asked questions, received answers regarding my participation in this study, and am willing to give consent for me to participate in this study. I will not have waived any of my rights by signing this consent form. Upon signing this consent form, I will receive a copy for personal records."

____
Name of Participant

____

____
Signature or mark of Participant Date

If a participant cannot read and or understand the form themselves, a witness must sign here:

I was present while the benefits, risks and procedures were read to the volunteer. All questions were answered and the volunteer has agreed to take part in the research.

____

Name of witness

____

____

Signature of witness / Mark Date

I certify that the nature and purpose, the potential benefits, and possible risks associated with participating in this research have been explained to the above individual.

____

Name of Person who Obtained Consent

____

____

Signature of Person Who Obtained Consent Date

Author details

Emmanuel Anongeba Anaba[1*], Juliana Gyasi Necku[2] and Moses Abile[3]

1 Department of Population, Family and Reproductive Health, University of Ghana, Accra, Ghana

2 37 Military Hospital, Accra, Ghana

3 Department of Nursing, Nursing and Midwifery Training College, Gushegu, Ghana

*Address all correspondence to: emmaanaba24@gmail.com

References

[1] Pernar CH et al. The epidemiology of prostate cancer. Cold Spring Harbor Perspectives in Medicine. 2018;**8**(12): a030361

[2] Center MM et al. International variation in prostate cancer incidence and mortality rates. European Urology. 2012;**61**(6):1079-1092

[3] Sauvé J-F, Lavoué J, Parent M-É. Occupation, industry, and the risk of prostate cancer: A case-control study in Montréal, Canada. Environmental Health. 2016;**15**(1):1-19

[4] Leavy J, Ambrosini G, Fritschi L. Vietnam military service history and prostate cancer. BMC Public Health. 2006;**6**(1):1-6

[5] Gan Y et al. Association between shift work and risk of prostate cancer: A systematic review and meta-analysis of observational studies. Carcinogenesis. 2018;**39**(2):87-97

[6] Zhu K et al. Cancer incidence in the US military population: Comparison with rates from the SEER program. Cancer Epidemiology and Prevention Biomarkers. 2009;**18**(6):1740-1745

[7] Joseph HJ. Determinants of prostate cancer screening in a sample of African American military servicemen. Military Medicine. 2006;**171**(5):430-435

[8] Oberst K et al. Work task disability in employed breast and prostate cancer patients. Journal of Cancer Survivorship. 2010;**4**(4):322-330

[9] Bradley CJ et al. Employment outcomes of men treated for prostate cancer. Journal of the National Cancer Institute. 2005;**97**(13):958-965

[10] Albaugh JA et al. Life after prostate cancer treatment: A mixed methods study of the experiences of men with sexual dysfunction and their partners. BMC Urology. 2017;**17**(1):1-9

[11] Arthur F et al. Prostate cancer screening in Ghana-a clinical benefit? Journal of Science and Technology (Ghana). 2006;**26**(1):1-7

[12] Clarke V, Braun V, Hayfield N. Thematic Analysis, Qualitative Psychology: A Practical Guide to Research Methods. London: SAGE Publications; 2015. pp. 222-248

[13] Appleton L et al. The impact of prostate cancer on men's everyday life. European Journal of Cancer Care. 2015;**24**(1):71-84

[14] Atinga RA, Yarney L, Gavu NM. Factors influencing long-term medication non-adherence among diabetes and hypertensive patients in Ghana: A qualitative investigation. PloS One. 2018;**13**(3):e0193995

[15] Houédé N et al. Impact on quality of life 3 years after diagnosis of prostate cancer patients below 75 at diagnosis: An observational case-control study. BMC Cancer. 2020;**20**(1):1-12

[16] Nabisubi P, Nanyingi M, Okeny PK. Lived experiences of prostate cancer patients below 55 years of age: A phenomenological study of outpatients receiving treatment at the Uganda cancer institute. East and Central African Journal of Surgery. 2020; **25**(3):1-13

[17] Watts S et al. Depression and anxiety in prostate cancer: A systematic review and meta-analysis of prevalence rates. BMJ Open. 2014;**4**(3):1-9

[18] Montazeri A. Health-related quality of life in breast cancer patients: A bibliographic review of the literature from 1974 to 2007. Journal of Experimental & Clinical Cancer Research. 2008;**27**(1):32

[19] Lee TK et al. Impact of prostate cancer treatment on the sexual quality of life for men-who-have-sex-with-men. The Journal of Sexual Medicine. 2015;**12**(12):2378-2386

[20] Roehrborn CG, Black LK. The economic burden of prostate cancer. BJU International. 2011;**108**(6):806-813

[21] Knaul FM et al. Self-identity, lived experiences, and challenges of breast, cervical, and prostate cancer survivorship in Mexico: A qualitative study. BMC Cancer. 2020;**20**(1):1-11

Section 5

Role of Birth Attendants

Chapter 6

Role of Community-Based Birth Attendants in Reduction of Maternal and Child Mortality

Mary Agoyi, Roland Ojo, Toyosi Afolabi, Olakunmi Ogunyemi, Sekinat Adejumobi and Adeyemi Awoniyi

Abstract

Community-based Birth Attendants (CBAs) provide maternal, child, sexual and reproductive information and services to a large part of the population in rural, marginalised and hard-to-reach communities (especially in underdeveloped and developing regions). In Nigeria, they cater for ~70% of the reproductive population who patronise them in their various communities due to accessibility, affordability and social acceptance for pregnancy-related care, delivery, other sexual and reproductive healthcare concerns. CBAs could be skilled, semiskilled but are largely unskilled. Their level of skill, knowledge, attitude, and practice in their community concerning different health issues is a huge determinant of their clients' health outcomes, which has also been skewed over time. Studies have shown that the knowledge of these CBAs continues to be impeded despite attempts at training them and unifying their practices, due to the deep-seated disunity that affects their uptake of thought interventions. These divisions are drawn along the lines of religion, initial training/education and gender differences. Therefore, continuous education on safe and current hygienic practices; increases their capacity, knowledge and skills for correct information dissemination and service delivery. Likewise, future assimilation into the formal health system with legal framework will help regulate their practices, thereby reducing maternal and child morbidity and mortality.

Keywords: maternal & child mortality, perinatal care, access to health, public health, community-based birth attendants, traditional birth attendants, community health, socioeconomic condition

1. Introduction

Maternal health, which is a core part of women's health during pregnancy, childbirth and the postpartum period, contributes massively to attaining an optimal public health state, as women make up half of the world's population and economies for development [1].

Pregnancy and childbirth should be joyous experiences for every woman and her household. However, this is not the case for some families as the joy is cut short at delivery, and a joyous occasion becomes a tragedy. Beyond the family, these deaths have detrimental effects on the socio-economic aspects of a country and the world at large [2].

Several factors contribute to these deaths, which are caused chiefly by the lack of appropriate care during pregnancy, childbirth, and post-delivery periods, with the bedrock of these care ingrained in the community. Community-based Birth Attendants (healthcare providers) provide this care for approximately 7 out of 10 women of reproductive age [3, 4].

2. Maternal and child mortality: incidence, causes and implications

Maternal mortality is defined as the loss of a woman's life resulting from pregnancy complication or death with 42 days after childbirth, notwithstanding the period or site of the pregnancy, emanating from issues that are linked or escalated by the management of the pregnancy but from accidental or incidental causes. Whereas, Early childhood mortality include Neonatal mortality (the probability of a child dying within the first month), Infant mortality (the probability of dying before the first birthday), Post-neonatal mortality (the difference between infant and neonatal mortality), Child mortality (the probability of dying between the first and the fifth birthday) and Under-5 mortality (the probability of dying between birth and the fifth birthday) [5].

Every year, women's lives are lost to complications of childbirth and pregnancy. According to the World Health Organisation, in 2017, 810 women died every day from preventable causes related to pregnancy and childbirth, with 94% of these deaths occurring in low and lower middle-income countries. In Nigeria, maternal mortality is reported to be 545 deaths per 100,000 live births and is currently known to have the second-highest number of maternal mortality (making up approximately 20% of all global maternal mortality) and perinatal mortality in the world, with unskilled TBAs assisting up to 90% of the deliveries that lead to these high statistics [4, 5].

Maternal deaths are due to complications that arise either during pregnancy or as a result of childbirth. While some conditions may exist before the pregnancy, the state of pregnancy can potentially worsen them. According to the WHO's International Classification of Diseases-Maternal Mortality (WHO ICD-MM), maternal deaths can be direct, indirect or unspecified [4, 5].

The direct causes are those resulting from obstetric complications of the pregnancy state, be it pregnancy, labour, or puerperium), including those related to interventions, omissions of treatment, or a combination of all. These include unsafe abortions, obstructed labour, excessive blood loss, infections. On the other hand, indirect deaths result from previously existing diseases or diseases developed in the pregnancy state that was aggravated by the physiologic effects of pregnancy. These include anaemia, high blood pressure and sugar, malaria, heart disease [4, 5].

However, according to Odeyemi et al. [6] also Maduka and Ogu [7], the common most reported causes of maternal deaths in Nigeria, direct and indirect, are obstetric haemorrhage leading to anaemia, pregnancy-induced hypertension, obstructed labour, unsafe abortion, ectopic pregnancy, placenta abruptio, ruptured uterus and puerperal sepsis.

Other unspecified maternal deaths are those during pregnancy, childbirth or puerperium for which the underlying cause cannot be determined. These are further divided into nine groups, which are; Pregnancies with abortive outcomes; Hypertensive disorders in pregnancy, childbirth and the puerperium; Obstetric haemorrhage; Pregnancy-related infection such as Human immunodeficiency virus/acquired immunodeficiency syndrome, and malaria; Other obstetric Complications; Unanticipated complications of management; Non-obstetric complications; Unknown/undetermined and finally, Coincidental causes [6, 7].

When women die, there are social and economic consequences that extend beyond her family. For the children left behind, evidence shows increased mortality risk, decreased nutrition and higher chances of not going to school. There is also the consequence of a reduced labour force for the community, which results in reduced productivity. There is evidence to show that maternal mortality has a statistically significant negative effect on GDP in the WHO African region [1, 2, 8].

In most instances, maternal deaths are preventable. This is possible through timely management of mothers by skilled professionals in an environment that is supportive and adequately equipped. Skilled professionals in this context are not limited to doctors, nurses or midwives. They include those health workers who live within the community, such as the Community-based Birth Attendants (CBAs) and other healthcare providers [9, 10].

3. CBAs as a strategy to reduce maternal and child mortality

Traditional birth attendant (TBA), which makes up the large part of CBAs, according to the World Health Organisation, is a person (usually a woman) who assists a pregnant woman at childbirth; she may have acquired her skills by delivering her babies alone or by working with other TBAs. Other groups also classified and acting as CBAs are CHOs, CHEWs, JCHEWs, auxiliary nurses, including faith-based birth attendants and even some trained midwives and nursing officers who offer service at homes and in the communities away from health facilities. In contrast, a trained or skilled TBA "is an individual who has received a form of short course training to enhance his/her knowledge and skills through the modern health care sector [11].

Over 50% of the 130 million deliveries globally are attended to by Community-based and Traditional birth attendants. These Community-based healthcare providers are largely unskilled (i.e. TBAs) and have no formal education or knowledge on the management of childbirth-related complications, while some are semiskilled or with outdated skills (i.e. auxiliary nurses) and, therefore, are unable to prevent or treat these complications during pregnancy or childbirth that leads to maternal and/or perinatal morbidities and mortalities [7, 12].

Significantly, Women of reproductive age living in developing and underdeveloped areas with weak health systems and suboptimal healthcare delivery – accounting for 94% of all maternal mortality globally where an estimate of about 45% of the death occurred during pregnancy; 35% during childbirth, and 20% during the postpartum period – continue to make use of TBAs during childbirth. This causes a negative ripple effect, with the unideal, inappropriate and unethical practice steadily increasing [6, 7].

Even though reports have shown a reduction in the maternal mortality rate over the years, this reduction rate has been very slow. The 2018 National Demographic Health Survey from Nigeria showed that skilled providers assisted 68% of births in urban areas compared with only 28% in rural areas, leaving the remaining 72% to the help of other unskilled Community-based Birth Attendants (CBAs) and other healthcare providers. Also, the study reflected that about 60% of the women in rural areas had a problem with accessing healthcare. These gaps highlight the importance of the availability of skilled community to women needing their services the most for necessary care [5].

A study done by Fagbamigbe et al. in 2017, to identify the cause of the marginal decline in maternal mortality rate in Nigeria identified an increased use in skilled birth attendants during delivery. The study showed a 6% increment in the use of skilled birth attendants between 1990 and 2013. The World Health Organisation also recorded a drop in maternal mortality rate by 53% during that period. Some of the factors responsible for the increased rate of skilled birth attendants use include creating the national midwives' service scheme, equipping primary health care centres, providing empowerment programs, and so on. Other determinants affecting women's usage of skilled birth attendants include proximity to the health facility, socio-economic status, and previous positive experience [4, 9].

Regarding health equity, the role of community birth attendants also comes to mind as they help ensure that women in rural communities are not left behind in terms of their maternal health care. Aside from being instrumental and playing a massive role in reducing maternal mortality, they also provide certain personalised care for their patients such as; counselling, home visitations, support during labor, charging cheaper rates, and allowing for payment of services by barter or in instalments. This is quite important for most women as a report has shown that the perception of skilled birth attendants as being hostile and disclosing confidential information are some of the hindering factors to receiving care from skilled birth attendants. Therefore, to significantly reduce the burden of maternal mortality in Nigeria, the role of the CBAs is of crucial importance and cannot be undermined [9, 11, 12].

4. Integration of CBAs in health service provision

The UN sustainable development goal to reduce the global maternal mortality ratio to <70 per 100,000 live births by 2030 seems impossible due to the prevalence of high maternal mortality rate globally (211 deaths per 100,000 live births in 2017) and in developing countries, especially Nigeria where there were about 917 deaths per 100,000 births in 2017. This is a product of these places' weak operational health systems – lacking well-trained, adequately informed, technology and quality inclined healthcare providers, well-maintained and equipped facilities, logistics and functional policies. Likewise, studies have shown that the risk of maternal and perinatal death is increased dramatically when there is unskilled birth assistance (done mainly by TBAs and other CBAs) [7].

The health workforce is the bedrock to achieving a good health system and its outcome. Hence, every healthcare provider, including the CBAs – who are a link between the community and health service providers especially, skilled birth attendants, and are always available, accessible, affordable and socioculturally acceptable in communities (especially the low socio-economic, rural, underserved, hard-to-reach and grassroots) – cannot be ruled out of the optimal healthcare provision and human resources allocation [9, 11–15].

Due to this, including the slow uptake and shortage of SBAs, several countries have opened up the proposal to officially adopt CBAs as part of the flowchart for maternity care and attempted to integrate CBAs into their health system – following the failure to suppress them. However, the results and techniques have differed from LMIC like Bangladesh and Kenya to HIC like China. Nevertheless, studies have shown that health education and training programs for TBAs are instrumental in upskilling them to promptly recognise warning signs of emergencies and know when to transfer the woman to the hospital [7, 9, 11, 12, 16].

Integrating them into the health system in Nigeria is challenging because, despite the widespread acceptance and use of these service providers, they are illegal. This is one of the major bottlenecks in integrating them into health services. Due to this problem, they can only function within the limits of the law as referral points, points of community entry, and they can help prevent harm to the mother and child. However, there is not enough SBA in the country, and as a result, policies such as task shifting and sharing will need to be adjusted to reflect and accommodate the current circumstance [7, 12, 15, 16].

The first step has to eliminate this problem and recognise them legally with well-defined roles and limits to serve their communities. They can regularly report to the local government medical officers, primary health centres, or the public health board with frequent assessments and updated recertification training. Some of the Knowledge and skills for procedures needed to ensure safe delivery and maternal and perinatal survival are the proper use, and implementation of aseptic techniques, uterotonics, anticonvulsants, antibiotics, blood transfusion, and more is lacking among them. Therefore, they should be trained to prevent and recognise complications by teaching them significant aspects of maternal care, including Family planning (FP), Misoprostol Use, Measurement of blood loss, Antepartum care, normal labour, Postpartum care for mothers, Postnatal care for neonates and so on. However, very importantly, these knowledge and skills should be fashioned and effectively implemented to fit their cadre, strict community level duties, in line with the task shifting and sharing policy in Nigeria [6, 7, 10, 12, 15].

5. Presumptive actions of CBAs in maternal healthcare service delivery

In the majority of the countries most affected by maternal mortality, uptake of family planning is low. Given that the CBAs are usually respected voices or authorities in their community, training them on family planning counselling and making them advocates will make it more appealing to the women. There is also a personal relationship and closeness between CBAs and their patrons still largely absent in the typical hospital or clinic dynamic. A reduction in the number of birthing events correlated strongly with a decrease in maternal deaths [15, 17].

Years ago, the prevention or treatment of postpartum haemorrhage in small villages or towns without electricity or the need for injections was near impossible. For example, in LMICs like Tanzania, they estimate blood loss using the quantity of soaked clothes fabrics and can be taught other standardised methods that are excellent steps at spotting postpartum haemorrhage. They can learn the local equivalence of 500mls of blood to know when to refer the women for advanced and emergency care in health facilities. Also, with the advent of misoprostol, it is possible to train these CBAs to administer it safely in their centres. This will reduce the risk of death due to postpartum haemorrhage, reducing one of the most emergent causes of maternal mortality [15, 18, 19].

CBAs can also encourage their patrons to get advanced care after birth and take vaccines in health centres. These are aspects of care that the majority of the CBAs generally do not offer in their regular plans, especially postpartum care. Notably, attempts to use "promise of financial compensation" to encourage the CBAs to refer their clients to the hospital for postpartum care have shown varying results. Teaching CBAs to clean women and care for them and their babies after delivery can save many lives lost to maternal and child mortality [14, 19].

Likewise, CBAs having good knowledge and counselling skills on HIV/AIDS and Prevention of Mother-To-Child Transmission of HIV (PMTCT) with good knowledge on specific measures of infection prevention and control can help them to protect themselves, their patients and the entire community while opting for orthodox medicine as the management of the various viral infection (COVID-19 inclusive), rather than the use of native or herbal remedies to cure them [18, 20].

All of these and more trainings, regular feedback, and a proper referral system will help create a genuinely integrated health service that has the interests of the healthcare consumers at the fore of its priorities. Hence, this is not the time to "gatekeep" but to be proactive by integrating CBAs via a full-on multifaceted project because human resources for health, including SBAs, are not growing fast enough to meet the community's needs. Therefore, all the stakeholders should be given a seat at the table to deliberate the methods, limits, appropriate policies and legislation [7, 13, 21].

6. Challenges and progress so far: discussion of field reports

Various challenges exist that hinder the maximisation of CBA roles to reduce maternal and child mortality and the general healthcare provision system as a whole. These challenges have been identified through an extensive review of literature and fieldwork.

Through our field works of Training-The-T/CBAs (Project TTT) at SHI, 162 CBAs has been reached since 2018, and some of the issues common to them all irrespective of location are palpable ignorance and reluctance to learn or adopt new methods. This reluctance is influenced by their confidence in their old traditional ways and how long they have been using them and getting away with the outcomes. For example, during the FGD on family planning before TTT at Orile-Iganmu (a Semi-Urban community in Lagos state, the megacity of Nigeria), the head of the TBAs (a herbalist) that has practised for over 30 years and trained countless other TBAs stated confidently in his native language and translated that *"BTL is tying of the cervix and meant for people that have done abortions in the past because their cervix and vagina have become wide and the "spring" there does not close. Therefore, the other forms of contraceptives like OCPs and condoms do not work for them..."*; whilst only 2 of the 162 CBAs reported that FP prevents (unsafe) abortion and none of them reported that FP prevents STIs in their pre-assessment questionnaires [22–24].

Also, other aspects found to be erroneously managed and discussed among them during an FGD among the same cohort and another recruited into the TTT Project in Ilo-Ajegunle (another semi-urban community in Lagos) were postpartum psychosis during and after labour, partners' inclusion in family planning, postdated pregnancy lasting up to one and half years, exclusive breastfeeding and other breastfeeding issues. Likewise, immunisation of mother and child and efficient data collection of their activities with the client were also lacking among the majority (**Tables 1–3**) [22–24].

Another occurrence was during the FGM session at the same training in Osogbo (the capital of the traditional and religious state), where more than 80% of the participant CBAs vehemently supported that FGM was a compulsory family tradition and right to protect the female. Also that they relied on their "*Opele*" – divining

TTT project location	Community type	State	C/TBAs recruited by
Osogbo	Semiurban	Osun	Traditional and TBAs leader
Orile-Iganmu	Semiurban	Lagos	Traditional and TBAs leader
Ilo-Ajegunle	Semiurban	Lagos	OIC and CHO in the community PHC
Ifako-Ijaiye	Semiurban	Lagos	CHO in the community PHC
Ojokoro	Semiurban	Lagos	CHO in the community PHC
Onipanu-Ota	Rural	Ogun	TBAs representative
Baale-Ajuwon	Rural	Ogun	Faith-based/Religious birthing attendants head

Table 1.
Details of field work (project locations) and methods through which C/TBAs trained were mobilised and recruited.

Age group	% (n = 162)
18–35 years	11.2
36–45 years	33.6
46–65 years	51.5
Above 65 years	3.7
Gender	% (n = 162)
Male	21.50
Female	78.50
Highest educational level	% (n = 162)
Primary education	21.4
Secondary education	46.8
Postsecondary education/Tertiary/Colleges	14.7
Informal or no education	17.1
Type of initial training had to become a TBA	% (n = 162)
Formally trained	52
Informally trained	48

NB: n is total number of Birthing Attendants reached by the TTT Project.
Data collection was by self-administered semi structured questionnaire, interview based and Focused Group Discussions. Data collation was between January 2018 till March 2021.

Table 2.
Sociodemographic data of birthing attendants (community-based/traditional) reached.

Cadre of birthing attendants reached (n = 162)	%
TBAs	38.00
CBAs	11.70
Faith Based	33.10
Nursing Officers	1.30
Auxiliary Nurses	12.70
JCHEWs	1.30
CHOs	1.30
CHEWs	0.60

NB: n is total number of Birthing Attendants reached by the TTT Project.

Table 3.
Cadre of the birthing attendants reached via the TTT.

oracle – and herbs for complex and prolonged/obstructed deliveries rather than refer to a health facility, which has been working for them. However, the untold consequences of these actions and strong beliefs are the morbidity and mortality cases recorded among the mothers and babies that patronise them when they return home to commence their everyday lives. Some of the highlighted morbidity outcomes in the babies leading to permanent damages are neonatal jaundice, mismanagement of the first golden minute of life. While in the mothers are puerperal sepsis, postpartum haemorrhage, to mention a few [22–25].

Furthermore, another challenge was the lack of a comprehensive and all-inclusive database of every functioning CBAs in communities despite having a regulating body or a converging association or point of meeting with their assigned CHOs in their resident community PHCs. Hence, they cannot all be tracked, trained, or their activities monitored, with some even hiding under the guise of running a "private hospital" instead of the actual traditional homes or centres they run. These can be due to age, level of exposure, type and level of education/training, the difference in religion, location/locality, beliefs and practices [24–26].

Some evidence supporting this from data collated through our TTT project showed that of the 162 reached and trained; 51.5% were between the ages of 46–65, 33.6% between 36 and 45 years, rarely the elderly who trained them showed (they made up only 3.7%) and the young one who are currently receiving the informal training (18–35 years' participant made up just 11.2%). Keep in mind that age should not be a limitation to acquiring knowledge. Likewise, primarily those who had some form of formal training wanted more, as 52.0% of participants had some formal training to become birth attendants or community healthcare providers versus 48.0% who were informally trained. While 21.4% had primary education, 46.8% had secondary education, 14.7% had postsecondary education (including college of health technology), and 17.1% had informal or no education [24].

Furthermore, the percentage of all participants attending the training by qualification and initial training recorded; 38.0% were TBAs, 33.1% faith-based birth attendants, 12.7% Auxiliary nurses, 11.7% CBAs, 1.3% Nursing Officers, 1.3% CHOs, 1.3% JCHEWs and 0.6% CHEW (SHI 2020 Annual report) [24]. This lower attendance of CBAs with higher qualifications might be attributed to the perceived need or aim of more training, mode of community entry, reachable circle and target of CBAs mobiliser [23, 24].

At a community entry meeting with one of the CBAs by the SHI strategy team (i.e. the contact person we were able to reach) in Baale-Ajuwon (a rural community in Ogun state), she emphasised in her native language that *"as a faith-based CBA, I try not to mingle with the TBAs because of their diabolic ways..."*, hence for the training would only reach out to the faith-based CBA like herself. This also shows the disharmony between the cadres of CBAs hindering them from learning and benefiting from each other to progress and be able to offer the best to their clients. Also participant sex percentage was 21.5% male to 78.5% female. It was found that where women were the CBA leaders, mostly women only tend to come for the trainings and be more expressive, as opposed to where men were the leaders - the meetings were more dominated by men with women less expressive and taking permission from the men to air their opinions [22–24]. This shows the gender disparity and inequality even at the level of community health care.

However, despite these challenges hindering their roles, some progress has been made such as the increase in the knowledge and attitude towards FP, Safe delivery, hygiene practices in the workspace, immunisation, exclusive breastfeeding and empowerment with IEC and educative materials for themselves and their clients; all of which play a huge role in reducing maternal and child morbidity and mortality in their communities and the world at large. As during follow-up visits to the CBAs in FDG, they report more patronage on account of the free birthing kits and FP counselling services they offer – courtesy of the Safer Hands Health Initiative [22–26].

7. The future and CBAS: recommendations

Currently and in the nearest future, the "irreplaceable" roles of CBAs in healthcare delivery services cannot be dismissed or disregarded. Hence, prompt actions must be taken to reduce the maternal, perinatal and child morbidity and mortality in Nigeria and globally associated with them. Some of which include;

Legalising the roles of CBAs and building a controlled framework to integrate them into the formal healthcare system. Also, incorporating community stakeholders input and participation can help improve healthcare service delivery and programs [7, 12, 13].

Strengthening effective communication between CBAs and skilled health workers to avoid disharmony and counter-productivity in the grassroots healthcare system. This can be achieved by creating a conducive and functional referral system and emergency line for CBAs to their community healthcare centres or medical practitioners in charge. This would also increase their access to healthcare facilities.

Trainings, educational conferences and empowerment at all levels (local, national and international) should be periodically and continuously done to cross-learn from what is obtainable and yield positive outcomes in other developed places. Also, with a day dedicated to them (i.e. International day of CBAs) to recognise their ethical works, referrals and reported/documented activities [16, 19, 24]. This would inform their activities, exposure and incline them towards quality care delivery.

Likewise, incentivising their efforts to recruit a robust database of every CBAs in their communities – as they know themselves – and enrol their trainees for proper/formal healthcare training in schools. Incentives could be per referral/enrollment or after a target number set is met, and it could be in the form of money, materials, or more opportunities like scholarships for formal enrollment, training, and attachment in recognised institutions [16, 19, 24]. This would encourage them to come out, be trained and get acquainted with policies, protocols, infrastructural and healthcare advancements. Owing to that fact that over 50% of the TTT participants reported that government policies had no impact on their activities and approximately 40% had no idea of any government policies affecting their work, while only about 9% reported that the government was putting in some efforts to make their works good but can still do better [22–24].

Finally, increasing quality community health education for women, men and their families – which are socioculturally appropriate and sensitive – is essential. As this would inform their healthcare decisions, improve their health-seeking behaviours, and positively influence paternal attitudes towards healthcare which is also an important factor for the overall well-being and economic status of women and their families [14, 17, 18, 26].

8. Conclusion

Birth attended by CBAs, especially TBAs, is associated more with maternal and child morbidity and mortality in Nigeria and globally, as most TBAs are unskilled. Currently, Nigeria is leading in maternal and child morbidity and mortality with the high patronage of TBAs as opposed to a skilled birth attendant or going to health facilities. Therefore, to reduce these maternal and perinatal deaths and, in turn, achieve the global Sustainable Development Goals (SDGs), it is pertinent to upscale the role of these CBAs for more skilled birth attendance and other delivery services by training them and possibly integrating them into the formal health system.

Acknowledgements

The author(s) would like to acknowledge the entire members of the CBA groups reached out to across various communities for making this possible, the CHOs and

IOC who served as mobilizers, Prof. Kofo Odeyemi for her continuous supervision of the project, Dr. Doyin Ogunyemi for her contributions and Birthing Kit Foundation Australia (BFKA) for their continuous provision of birthing kits used as incentives for the CBAs.

Conflict of interest

The authors declare no conflict of interest.

Thanks

Thanks to every partner, strategy team members and volunteers of Safer Hands Health Initiative, for the collation of data and being an integral part of this project.

Appendices and nomenclature

CBAs	Community-based birth attendants
TBAs	Traditional birth attendants
SBAs	Skilled birth attendants
OIC	Officer in charge
CHOs	Community health officers
PHCs	Primary healthcare centres
CHEWs	Community health extension workers
JCHEWs	Junior Community health extension workers
TTT	Training the traditional/community-based birth attendants
SDGs	Sustainable development goals
FP	Family planning
BTL	Bilateral tubal ligation
FGM	Female genital mutilation
GDP	Gross domestic profit
STIs	Sexually transmitted infections
WHO	World health organisation
SHI	Safer hands health initiative
LMICs	Low middle income countries
HICs	High-income countries
FGD	Focused group discussion

Author details

Mary Agoyi*, Roland Ojo, Toyosi Afolabi, Olakunmi Ogunyemi, Sekinat Adejumobi and Adeyemi Awoniyi
Safer Hands Health Initiative, Lagos, Nigeria

*Address all correspondence to: kemisolaagoyi@gmail.com

References

[1] Olonade O, Olawande TI, Alabi OJ, Imhonopi D. Maternal mortality and maternal health care in Nigeria: Implications for socio-economic development. Open Access Maced J Med Sci. 2019;**7**(5):849-855

[2] Molla M, Mitiku I, Worku A, Yamin AE. Impacts of maternal mortality on living children and families: A qualitative study from Butajira Ethiopia. Reproductive Health. 2015;**12**(1):S6

[3] Ebuehi OM, Akintujoye I. Perception and utilization of traditional birth attendants by pregnant women attending primary health care clinics in a rural Local Government Area in Ogun State Nigeria. International Journal of Women's Health. 2012;**4**:25-34

[4] World Health Organization. Maternal Mortality [Internet] . [cited 2021 Nov 13]. Available from: https://www.who.int/news-room/fact-sheets/detail/maternal-mortality

[5] Nigeria National Population Commission (NPC) and International Coaching Federation (ICF) 'Nigeria Demographic and Health Survey (NDHS) 2018 Key Indicators Report', Abuja, Nigeria, and Rockville, Maryland, USA. [Internet]. 2019 . [cited 2021 May 13]. Available from: http://cs-sunn.org/wp-content/uploads/2018/10/NDHS-2018.pdf

[6] Odeyemi K, Abidoye G, Akin-Adenekan O, Akinsola O, Ekanem E, Osilaja O, et al. Causes of maternal mortality in Lagos State. Nigeria. Annals of Tropical Medicine and Public Health. 2014;7:177

[7] Maduka O, Ogu R. Preventing Maternal Mortality During Childbirth: The Scourge of Delivery with Unskilled Birth Attendants [Internet]. Childbirth. IntechOpen; 2020. [cited 2021 Nov 13]. Available from: https://www.intechopen.com/chapters/70849

[8] Kirigia JM, Oluwole D, Mwabu GM, Gatwin D, Kainyu LH. Effects of maternal mortality on gross domestic product (GDP) in the WHO African region. Afri J Health Sci. 2006;**13**:86-95

[9] Fagbamigbe AF, Hurricane-Ike EO, Yusuf OB, Idemudia ES. Trends and drivers of skilled birth attendant use in Nigeria (1990-2013): Policy implications for child and maternal health. International Journal of Women's Health. 2017;**9**:843-853

[10] Okereke E, Ishaku SM, Unumeri G, Mohammed B, Ahonsi B. Reducing maternal and newborn mortality in Nigeria—a qualitative study of stakeholders' perceptions about the performance of community health workers and the introduction of community midwifery at primary healthcare level. Human Resources for Health. 2019;**17**(1):102

[11] Ogbo FA, Trinh FF, Ahmed KY, Senanayake P, Rwabilimbo AG, Uwaibi NE, et al. Prevalence, trends, and drivers of the utilization of unskilled birth attendants during democratic governance in Nigeria from 1999 to 2018. International Journal of Environmental Research and Public Health. 2020;**17**(1):372

[12] Sulayman H, Adaji S. Integration of traditional birth attendants (TBAs) into the health sector for improving maternal health in Nigeria: A systematic review. Sub-Saharan African Journal of Medicine. 2019;**6**(2):55-62

[13] Wilunda C, Dall'Oglio G, Scanagatta C, Segafredo G, Lukhele BW, Takahashi R, et al. Changing the role of traditional birth attendants in Yirol West County South Sudan. PLoS One. 2017;**12**(11):e0185726. DOI: 10.1371/journal.pone.0185726

[14] Envuladu EE, Agbo HA, Lassa S, Kigbi JH, Zoakah AI. Factors determining the choice of a place of delivery among pregnant women in Russa village of Jos North, Nigeria; achieving the MDGs 4 and 5. Int J Med Biomed Res. 2013;**2**:23-29

[15] Prata N, Passano P, Rowen T, Bell S, Walsh J, Potts M. Where there are (few) skilled birth attendants. Journal of Health, Population, and Nutrition. 2011;**29**(2):81-91. DOI: 10.3329/jhpn.v29i2.7812

[16] Kitui JE, Dutton V, Bester D, et al. Traditional Birth Attendant reorientation and Motherpacks incentive's effect on health facility delivery uptake in Narok County, Kenya: An impact analysis. BMC Pregnancy and Childbirth. 2017;**17**(125). DOI: 10.1186/s12884-017-1307-7

[17] Olakunde BO, Adeyinka DA, Mavegam BO, Olakunde OA, Yahaya HB, Ajiboye OA, et al. Factors associated with skilled attendants at birth among married adolescent girls in Nigeria: Evidence from the Multiple Indicator Cluster Survey, 2016/2017. International Health. 2019;**11**(6):545-550

[18] Olufunke F, Olajumoke A, Andy EC, Omolara D, Katherine K, Andrew S, et al. Applying a Client-centered approach to maternal and neonatal networks of care: Case studies from urban and rural Nigeria. Health Systems & Reform. 2020;**6**:2. DOI: 10.1080/23288604.2020.1841450

[19] Chukwuma A, Mbachu C, McConnell M, et al. The impact of monetary incentives on referrals by traditional birth attendants for postnatal care in Nigeria. BMC Pregnancy and Childbirth. 2019;**19**(150):150. DOI: 10.1186/s12884-019-2313-8

[20] Balogun M, Odeyemi K. Knowledge and practice of prevention of mother-to-child transmission of HIV among traditional birth attendants in Lagos State, Nigeria. The Pan African Medical Journal. 2010;**5**:7

[21] WHO. WHO Integrating health services WHO/HIS/SDS/2018.50 [Internet]. 2018 . Available from: https://www.who.int/docs/default-source/primary-health-care-conference/linkages.pdf [Accessed: 13 Oct 2021]

[22] Agoyi MO. Training The Traditional Birth Attendants (TTT) Project [Internet]. 2020 . Available from: https://saferhandsinitiative.org/training-the-traditional-birth-attendants-ttt-project [Accessed: 13 Oct 2021]

[23] Agoyi MO. Hygienic Practices and Service Delivery of CBAs During The COVID-19 Pandemic Project [Internet]. 2020 . Available from: https://saferhandsinitiative.org/hygienic-practices-and-service-delivery-of-cbas-during-the-covid-19-pandemic-2 [Accessed: 13 Oct 2021]

[24] Safer Hands Health Initiative Annual Report 2020 [Internet]. 2021 . Available from: https://saferhandsinitiative.org/reports [Accessed: 13 Oct 2021]

[25] Safer Hands Health Initiative. TBAs: The ones there, when we are not [Internet]. 2021 . Available from: https://saferhandsinitiative.org/tbas-the-ones-there-when-we-are-not [Accessed: 13 Oct 2021]

[26] Amutah-Onukagha N, Rodriguez M, Opara I, Gardner M, Assan MA, Hammond R, et al. Progresses and challenges of utilizing traditional birth attendants in maternal and child health in Nigeria. International Journal of MCH and AIDS. 2017;**6**(2):130-138. DOI: 10.21106/ijma.204

www.ingramcontent.com/pod-product-compliance
Lightning Source LLC
LaVergne TN
LVHW081932200926
848484LV00009B/2409